Features
and Fillers

Texas Journalists on
Texas Folklore

Publications of the Texas Folklore Society LVI

Jim Harris, Editor
Carolyn Satterwhite, Assistant Editor

Francis Edward Abernethy, General Series Editor

University of North Texas Press
Denton, Texas

Printed in the United States of America

Requests for permission to reproduce material from
this work should be sent to:

Permissions
University of North Texas Press
PO Box 311336
Denton TX 76203-1336
940-565-2142

The paper in this book meets the minimum requirements of the
American National Standard for Permanence of Paper for
Printed Library Materials, Z39.48.1984

Library of Congress Cataloging-in-Publication Data

Features and fillers : Texas journalists on Texas folklore / Jim Harris, editor.
p.   cm. — (Publications of the Texas Folklore Society ; 56)
Includes index.
ISBN 1-57441-074-1 (alk. Paper)
1. Folklore—Texas. 2. Folklore—Texas—Press coverage.
3. American newpapers—Texas. I. Harris, Jim, 1942–   .
II. Series: Publications of the Texas Folklore Society ; no. 56.
GR1.T4 no. 56
[GR110.T4]
398".09764—dc21   99-16387
                               CIP

Design by Angela Schmitt

Contents

vii Dedication
Paul Patterson

1 Texas Journalists on Texas Folklore
Jim Harris

17 A Legend Runs Through It
Bryan Woolley *The Dallas Morning News*

30 The Weeping Woman
John O. West *The Fort Worth Star-Telegram*

37 Bois d'Arc Recollections
Ernestine and Charles Linck *The Commerce Journal*

44 Prescriptions for Ailments Did Not Always Find a Cure *and* Dyin' Easy and Several Other Ways of Crossing Over and Departing This Life
Joyce Gibson Roach *The Fort Worth Star-Telegram*

51 Musing on Distant, Faded Glories of the Days of Radio
Robert J. Duncan *The Fort Worth Star-Telegram*

55 Unknowingly, Security Guard Takes on KKK
Robert J. Duncan *McKinney Courier Gazette*

58 Four Musings on Bad Roosters
Henry Wolff, Jr. *The Victoria Advocate*

66 The Ol' Red Rooster Learns a Hard Lesson
Lora B. Garrison *Uvalde Leader-News*

70 Hallie Stillwell Will Live on in Memories
Kent Biffle *The Dallas Morning News*

75 Ex-Sheriff's Tale Is One for History Books
Kent Biffle *The Dallas Morning News*

80 Tales of a Rural School Teacher
Lou Rodenberger   *The Fort Worth Star-Telegram*

85 The New Year Hasn't Always Started January 1;
Valentine's Day: How It All Began; *and*
Columbus Day Roots Are in This Century
Archie McDonald   *The Daily Sentinel*

93 Texas' Oddest Animal
Jerry Turner   *The Mexia Daily News*

96 What Mrs. Rives Found in Gilmer
Sarah Greene   *The Gilmer Mirror*

102 He 'Woodn't' Trade Hobby for Anything
John Fooks   *The Texarkana Gazette*

106 The Ghosts of Bill Longley; Bill Longley on the
Gallows; *and* Haunted by Bill Longley
A. C. Greene   *The Dallas Morning News*

113 Weather Lore Isn't All Wet
Stanley Marcus   *The Dallas Morning News*

115 Animals Dominate Our Language
Stanley Marcus   *The Dallas Morning News*

118 Brilliant Brickmanship
Allan Turner   *Houston Chronicle*

124 History as Close as a Turntable
Allan Turner   *Houston Chronicle*

137 Working Hard, Joking Hard on the Frontier
Lawrence Clayton   *Dallas Times Herald*

142 Cow Chip Tea
Haywood Hygh   *Marshall News Messenger*

153 Orient Hotel Saw Good Times and Bad
Elmer Kelton   *West Texas Livestock Weekly*

158 *El Ojo* and Other Folk Beliefs
Joe Graham   *The Fort Worth Star-Telegram*

164 The Cleo Face
Mike Cox   *San Angelo Standard-Times*

168 Dr. J. Mason Brewer
James W. Byrd   *The Commerce Journal*

172 Dusting Out
Francis Edward Abernethy   *Dallas Times Herald*

178 Alfonso's Yearly Routine
T. Lindsay Baker   *Eagle-News*

181 Making the Rattlesnake Roundup Circuit
T. Lindsay Baker   *Eagle-News*

184 Rayon Dresses and FDR
T. Lindsay Baker   *The Clarendon News*

187 A Collection of Poems
Jean Schnitz   *The Kingsville-Bishop Record News*

195 Gold Diggers
Patrick Dearen   *The Midland Reporter-Telegram*

206 Chicken-fried Steak Tour through Texas
Alan Solomon   *Chicago Tribune*

213 Cowboy Poet Honored by Peers
Peggy McCracken   *Pecos Enterprise*

216 Telling "Tales" Keeps Patterson Busy and Happy
Rosie Flores   *Pecos Enterprise*

222 Contributors

229 Index

Dedication

The Texas Folklore Society
dedicates this book to Paul Patterson.

In ninety years of the Texas Folklore Society, rarely has the Society singled out a member and contributor for honor by dedicating one of its annual publications. But rarely does a man like ninety-year-old Paul Patterson come along. The Crane-Pecos, Texas, writer, teacher, storyteller, folklorist and humorist has been an inspiration for many Society members for more years than most folks can count.

The last publication with a dedication to an individual was *Hoein' the Short Rows*, 1987, which honored Martha Emmons. Like Miss Martha, Mr. Paul has served the Society with instruction and entertainment that will forever be part of the organization's traditions. He is a man we have laughed with and listened to while we have marveled at his wit and his insight.

Thanks, Paul.

Texas Journalists on Texas Folklore

Jim Harris

Several years ago I started writing a local history column for my hometown newspaper, the *Hobbs News-Sun*. I decided to call it "The Southwest" to give myself a broader range of topics, thinking that my sparsely-populated, rural area of Lea County in the southeastern corner of New Mexico and the adjacent counties in West Texas might be a little limiting in my choices of subject matter.

But I learned, as a full-time journalist would already have known, that small communities, even in rural regions, are filled with hundreds of stories. I learned that my niche in the Southwest contained narratives enough for me to write about for the rest of my life and for at least two or three more lives if I decided to come back in another form, say as a newspaper columnist.

I learned this lesson quickly because readers in my section of the Land of Enchantment—known as Little Texas—and readers in West Texas came forth to tell me so. They wrote, called, and stopped me in the grocery store to say they or their cousins or neighbors had a slice of history to pass along, and if I would just come by they would serve it to me so I could give it back to the rest of the folks in our area.

In fact, I found out soon that the readers in my territory were hungry for particular kinds of articles. They wanted narratives that had something to do with their distant and immediate past, but they did not want the histories they remembered from classrooms—listings of presidents, governors and mayors with dates of offices.

Readers were starving for stories they might hear in conversations over a glass of tea, stories about the Native Americans who once roamed the plains, settlers who came from the east, the formation of early 20th-century communities, abandoned school houses, how a ghost town got its name, an infamous stretch of county road, a famous ranch, ranch dances held in decades past, the cockfights held down in the southern part of the county, the old movie theater that closed in the 1950s, an old rodeo hand, a woman who lived in a dugout when she was a girl, life in the oil camps, and hunting for arrowheads below the caprock.

In other words, what the people in my region wanted to read

was not so much their *history* as their *folklore*, passed down through the years, much of it by word of mouth but some of it preserved and circulated by other means.

Since the 19th-century scholar W. J. Thoms created the word, just about everyone who has written of folklore has taken a crack at defining it, resulting in hundreds of definitions by experienced teachers and beginning students intent on creating the final words on the popular subject. I like the simple definition the late J. Mason Brewer gave to a group of young people in Commerce, Texas, in the early 1970s. Brewer said that folklore is the traditions, customs and practices of a given group of people. He went on to develop some of its characteristics, but there was enough in his brief definition to carry me through myriad folklore ponderings and discussions. Believing in the old maxim that there's no need to reinvent the wheel, I have repeated Brewer's definition scores of times and still find it satisfying.

Looking back at the folklore and history of my home in Little Texas, at the narratives of several small towns, some of them gone with few traces left, I found that certain traditions were passed along by the area newspapers and that those same papers often were conduits for the contemporary customs of the communities. It is not hard to imagine that they kept the people connected, giving the people a sense of belonging to a group when the distances between neighbors should have isolated them.

It is my guess that Texas newspapers have functioned that way for as long as there has been a Texas, and not just in rural and isolated regions of the state. Texas newspapers have fed and continue to feed their readers and their communities with local and state-wide traditional life.

Journalists use folklore subjects in a variety of ways, and traditions, customs and practices may appear in a newspaper in a variety of formats. For instance, a paper might simply report an upcoming folk event, a traditional festival. It might report as news the creation of a traditional artifact, an individual's rug or a communal quilt, for example. It might report on a local rumor, such as a tale about a jail breakout that prompted scores of calls to the local police but that turned out to be a tale circulating in other communities around the state.

Just last year, several papers and television and radio stations in New Mexico reported that the New Mexico State Police had received information that gang members in Albuquerque were driving around with their lights off, then chasing down and shooting at any car whose lights were flashed to warn the car without lights. In subsequent news reports, readers learned that the story had circulated some six years earlier and there were no specific motorists who had reported having had such an encounter with gangs. Probably, the state police suggested, it was just a rumor, what folklorists call a "modern urban legend."

Beyond news stories, newspapers offer folk materials in many other forms, some of them touted as folklore, some of them presented without folkloristic intent on the part of the journalists. A newspaper might publish a profile of a local folk artist, such as the self-taught musician who always plays in the area fiddle contests, or the woman who creates murals on the sides of buildings for local businesses.

Still another way that folklore appears in newspapers is in the writings and rewritings of familiar historical events. One of the oldest settlements in my county is called Monument, and there are several versions of the historical incidents that determined the town's name, including stories about the buffalo hunters who built a rock house at Monument Springs and stories about Colonel William Shafter who had his buffalo soldiers erect a rock pile to mark the location of the valuable waterhole. The Monument narratives got more complicated when in the 1930s a real estate promoter built a statue of a Native American—he called it Geronimo—to designate the site of wonderful investment opportunities. For later generations, this was "the" monument of the town. It would be no exaggeration to say that there has not been a year gone by in the latter half of the 20th century without some stories about Monument's name in the newspapers of Southeastern New Mexico.

The impact on traditional life of newspaper use of folk materials can range from the extremely positive (a newspaper might serve as a disseminator of traditions) to the very negative (it might spread fakelore among its readers).

In the past, conservative folklorists and scholars might have argued that once a tradition, such as a local legend or tale, enters the print media, it ceases to be folklore. But no one would argue against the fact that the legend or tale that came from the folk and was reported in the newspaper, might once again be part of the word-of-mouth body of lore passed among the people. A legend or tale may be altered somewhat when an informant learned of it first on the printed page, but variants are part and parcel of folklore, a quality that even the most conservative folklorists attribute to all customary life.

When considering modern folklore, some folklorists have gone far beyond the older thinking that all folklore must be passed on by word of mouth. In her 1994 book *Folklore and the Mass Media* (Indiana University Press) Linda Degh writes, "It is not enough to recognize that mass media play a role in folklore transmission. It is closer to the truth to admit that the media have become part of folklore."

But no matter what his or her personal beliefs about the definition of folklore, any observant reader of Texas newspapers will find examples of traditional life, in one form or another, being reported and analyzed in the state's papers, be they large circulation dailies in metropolitan areas, such as *The Dallas Morning News*, or small papers in rural and isolated regions, such as *The Pecos Enterprise*. The writers of these stories range from beginning reporters and part-time columnists, to veteran editors, and the subjects vary from a tale about the Alamo to trades day in Canton to building houses out of adobe in the Rio Grande Valley.

Just last year, a *Chicago Tribune* writer, Alan Solomon, traveled through Texas and wrote for his paper a story with the headline, "Chicken-Fried Steak Tour through Texas." The first person he quoted in his story was long-time Texas folklorist Joyce Roach, who is the author, along with Ernestine Sewell Linck, of *Eats, a Folk History of Texas Foods*.

Solomon's story was printed in several papers across the country, including *The Albuquerque Journal* where I read it. Like cream gravy over a good chicken fried steak, the article spread traditional Texas attitudes about what has been called the "national dish of Texas."

Solomon's article, I am sure, was intended to be a good-natured and humorous look at Texas eating habits, which may sound a little peculiar to Chicago residents dining along the banks of Lake Michigan. But it is not hard to imagine a young waitress in Waco passing along to her customers one of the humorous anecdotes Solomon related in his article. For instance, James M. White, owner of the Broken Spoke cafe and bar in Austin, is reported to have said, "Gravy and chicken-fried steak is like Bob Wills and western swing country music."

In the fall of last year, I spent a number of weeks examining big city and small town Texas and New Mexico newspapers for folklore content. For my informal analysis, I read *The Dallas Morning News* because at least two prominent Texas Folklore Society members, Kent Biffle and Bryan Woolley, write there. And I read several West Texas and Eastern New Mexico small town papers, such as *The Alpine Avalanche* and *The Lovington Leader*, because they happened to be handy. In addition, I continued to read and examine four area papers I have read regularly for the past twenty-five years: *The Lubbock Avalanche-Journal*, *The Odessa American*, *The Albuquerque Journal*, and *The Hobbs News-Sun*.

The small-town papers, it seems to me, offer more opportunities for writers to consider folklore subjects. Although *The Alpine Avalanche* may have a tough editor who demands a certain amount of national news in each issue, generally speaking his paper and other small papers welcome local news, and many of them insist on covering the local scene first and filling in with state and national news only when there is room. The local beat, with less pressure to cover the national or regional beat, offers many more opportunities to write about traditional and customary life found in the community.

For instance, the local history column, often written by a part-time journalist or one-time high school history teacher, is found in many small papers. In these columns, historical events are related as they are told within the community, some of them emphasizing what is traditionally passed along rather than what may be officially recorded in history texts. To take an atypical but fascinating example, the Fort Davis newspaper, *The Jeff Davis County Mountain Dispatch*, could fill every weekly issue with the hundreds of anecdotes—about Colonel William Shafter, the buffalo soldiers and fearsome Native Americans—that circulate in the isolated West Texas community that is the site of a famous frontier fort.

I would suspect that after the 1997 state trooper shootout with the Republic of Texas hooligans outside of Fort Davis, the little town will be abuzz for many decades to come with scores of other tales about what happened and didn't happen. At a family style cafe there following the nationally televised fracas, my wife and I had dinner with a local couple who told us that during the standoff they were more frightened of the hordes of policemen than they were of their Republic of Texas neighbors. It is not hard to imagine the potential for legend building in this small town, which I admit is not a typical Texas small town, and it is my guess that *The Mountain Dispatch* will play a role in keeping many of those narratives alive even after the current population has moved to that beautiful resort town in the sky.

The November 19, 1998, issue of *The Mountain Dispatch* carried a column by Nessye Mae Roach (no relation to Joyce Roach) called "Long Ago." The column title included a pen-and-ink drawing of a cowboy holding a rifle, a woman in a Victorian dress standing to the side and slightly behind him, and the fronts of four buildings of a frontier town. In the article, Ms. Roach wrote of the life of the governess in West Texas in the early 1900s. Without naming her, Roach wrote of one specific governess brought to a ranch to school the rancher's kids. The young lady found out that she was expected to clean house and do other chores in addition to her teaching duties, so after a few months she left the job when she realized the rancher ruled his home like a dictator and that the family was going to be taking advantage of her. Roach ended the article by saying the governess herself had told the story to the writer, and it had been verified by other people.

The message in Roach's article is that ranch life in the West of a century ago was hard on these young women, who were often treated poorly by the families who hired them. In fact, what the writer does pass along to the readers is another familiar narrative found in western folklore, fiction and film—the women who helped settle the West had rough lives, and many of them paid a price for their pioneer roles. It does not matter that by 1900 the West was supposed to be already settled; many folks in West Texas continue to think their country was still frontier far into the 20th century. There are numerous possibilities for Roach's article to impact the folklore of the Fort Davis community, with her version of the young governess's story being just one of many similar tales of the exploits of women in the West.

But it is not just on narratives that the small-town paper focuses in covering the local scene. There are stories about customary life, such as seasonal dances and craft fairs, and there are stories about local folk heroes. Stories about West Texas folklorist, cowboy poet, and writer Paul Patterson have appeared in many Texas newspapers. A couple of those stories appear in this book, and I am sure there is a thick scrapbook of Paul's news stories and features in somebody's hands.

The November 19, 1998, issue of *The Alpine Avalanche* carried several articles of interest to the folklorist. For one, a story with a two-column photograph announced that novelist and long-time Texas Folklore Society member Elmer Kelton would be in town over the weekend to sign copies of his new book *The Smiling Country.* The story begins, "West Texas' most loved author will be in Alpine Saturday." Much has been written about how popular fiction has influenced American folklore in the last 150 years, and Texans are aware of the influence of writers such as Kelton and Larry McMurtry in shaping traditional views of the state's past and present. In several ways, both of those writers are pipelines to the past and preservers of tradition; and they are like popular musicians whose compositions are variations on customary songs.

I recall a story I heard Kelton tell. A West Texas cowboy reads a western novel (or sees a western film) and spends the rest of his cowboy life walking and talking like John Wayne. I believe it was Elmer who told that story, or perhaps it was Max Evans or Paul Patterson.

Also appearing in *The Alpine Avalanche* was a story about Terlingua artist Crystal Marks who would be in town as part of Gallery Night '98, a festival emphasizing the appreciation and purchasing of local art. One headline read "Apache Trading Post Celebrating Twenty-two years of Offering Yuletide Treasures Saturday Night," and the story included expressions such as "in keeping with tradition." It is obvious that Alpine's Gallery Night, like its thirteen-year-old Texas Cowboy Poetry Gathering, is not a true folk festival but is the sort of Chamber of Commerce activity created in many communities to spur tourism and to prime the local economy. Many would not consider these activities a part of regional folklore. But there may be a point at which the commercial impulse and the folk practice dovetail into an event that does become part of local customary life. This has been the case with the burning of Zozobra (old man gloom) in Santa Fe, New Mexico, in the Fall. It may also be the case with drives to aid the poor and feed them a traditional meal in many towns and cities during the Thanksgiving and Christmas holidays. It may be too that Alpine's cowboy gathering will some day be such an integral part of Alpine's customary life that no one would *not* consider it folklore no matter how it originated. It is certain that West Texas area newspapers have played a big role in making the event as popular as it is today.

Newspapers larger than *The Alpine Avalanche* or Marfa's *The Big Bend Sentinel* but smaller than *The Houston Chronicle*, the so-called mid-sized Texas newspapers, offer their readers some of the advantages found in both the big and little papers. They can give the readers the small town's sense of community with appropriate subjects, and they can often support larger staffs with specialists in various newspaper genres. *The Lubbock Avalanche-Journal* is a good example of this type of newspaper. It circulates in much of West Texas and eastern New Mexico and tries to accommodate its readers in surrounding towns, such as Floydada, Levelland, Clovis, Hobbs, Seminole and Lamesa, with area coverage.

The Sunday, November 29, 1998, issue included a number of articles with a folk tilt to them. One story was about the 1927-built Turkey, Texas, hostelry in Bob Wills's home town. The issue also contained an Associated Press story, "American Folk Marquetry Is Finding Way into Home Design." And the Arts Section had two long stories by William Kerns headlined "Under the West Texas Sky," which profiled famed nature photographer Wyman Meinzer and included several good-looking color photos of the South Plains. I mention the Meinzer articles here because this is a photographer who seems to have been able to capture beautiful images of many icons of Texas folklore, such as the coyote and the roadrunner. I would wager that prints of his photographs will be on calendars and walls of many southwestern homes for years to come.

Annually *The Lubbock Avalanche-Journal* does extensive coverage and helps sponsor the town's own cowboy gathering, The National Cowboy Symposium, which celebrates in tale, song and poem traditional life on the ranch. This is an event attended by thousands of visitors from West Texas, from Eastern New Mexico and from many other states. When I attended the 1998 symposium, I was reminded of the State Fair of Texas I visited in the 1940s and 1950s.

A town the size of Lubbock can also support tabloid newspapers that cover such subjects as the local arts scene, local history and local religion. Lubbock's *Caprock Sun* carries reviews of art shows, movies and plays in town, and it publishes poems by local versifiers. In the December, 1998, issue the *Sun* had poems entitled "Good Friday" and "The Plowman," both of which might be thought of as folk poems. At the end of 1998, Lubbock also supported a small newspaper called *Lubbock County Independent,* a conservative publication which printed in its December 11 issue a column called "Men Bashing," which listed fifteen traveling anecdotes and jokes focusing on male inadequacies. An example: Why are blonde jokes so short? So men can remember them.

As for the larger circulation Texas papers, what they may lack in having close ties to a smaller, more uniform and more static community and readership, they make up by having staffs large enough to employ many feature writers and columnists. *The Dallas Morning News,* for instance, has columnists such as Kent Biffle, Bryan Woolley, and Bob St. John, who focus on various aspects of Texas history and contemporary life.

In the November 14, 1998, issue of the *News*, Bob St. John wrote about historic Jefferson Street in Dallas's Oak Cliff section. Jefferson Street was one of my stompin' grounds when I was a kid, and one of the places St. John wrote about was the Texas Theater where Lee Oswald was captured following the assassination of President Kennedy. As a youngster I saw dozens of movies at the Texas, including a film version of *Hamlet* in which Richard Burton played the indecisive Dane. Down the street from the Texas and just off Jefferson, I shot many a game of 8-ball in the Lancaster Club pool hall. So I associate Jefferson Street with many of the rites of passage city boys go through in their teens. In writing about this "historic district," St. John was really covering what might be called the "folk beat," meaning the subjects of his article are just as much traditional tales and traditional life as historical events.

In the same issue of the *Morning News* (November 14, 1998), and carried as straight news, was a story about internet messages warning computer users never to punch in telephone numbers over the phone because scam artists and other criminals can use the numbers to make their own calls and charges. The story revealed that the internet messages were just rumors, that no one had actually had this happen to them, and it would be extremely difficult for a criminal to pull it off. The writer of the news story announced that this was an example of a modern "legend" circulating in cyberspace—as other urban stories circulate by word of mouth. Thus, *The Dallas Morning News* passes along a tale about communicating on the telephone, but also a tale circulating on the world wide web. After reading the article, folklorists might have wondered about what would happen to the rumor when it entered an oral stage, as most likely it would since so much of office talk today centers on computers, the web and email.

Another offering the larger papers provide that smaller papers usually do not is the travel section. These sections generally appear in the Sunday editions, but individual travel stories get published throughout the week. Travel stories, it seems to me, offer many opportunities for the spreading of folklore to a larger audience. Before my wife and I traveled to Tahiti in August of 1998, we read newspaper travel pieces about life on the South Pacific islands, and usually the writers would try to emphasize the quaint, distinctive qualities of the people in the town of Papeete and on the islands of Bora Bora and Moorea. They wanted to give the flavor of the place, which meant sketching some of the folklife there. On the island of Tahiti, this included traditional houses, foods, occupations, and religious celebrations.

Travel features in the larger Texas papers can be grist for the state folklore mill by covering the customs of folks around such diverse settings as an historic hotel in Jefferson, the Strand district in Galveston, the Santa Ana National Wildlife Refuge outside McAllen, and the 19th-century cemetery in El Paso where John Wesley Hardin is buried.

Folklore subjects offer travel writers material that is immediately interesting to large numbers of readers and that can be insightful revelations about the people in places where tourists want to go. Travel articles do not offer the writer opportunities to go into great depth about the folklore of a particular place, but they can still open a window into the culture of a place and at the same time spread narratives about communities near and far.

In the Sunday, November 29, 1998, issue of my state newspaper, *The Albuquerque Journal*, Isaac Guzman wrote the text and took the photographs for a travel-section article called "Mexico's Heartland: Writer Reconnects with Family, Culture during Tour through Highlands." Guzman's piece turns out to be less of a geographic tour and more of a cultural journey in which the writer searches for his Mexican roots. Mexico travel pieces are particularly popular in Albuquerque because so many people who live there and in northern New Mexico have Mexican ties; many of them are recent arrivals in the United States. The Rio Grande is still a pipeline to the U. S. from El Paso del Norte in Texas, and for many along the river's northern sections a Mexican feature in the newspapers is a means of staying in touch with their homes along the southern portions of the Rio Bravo, the Mexican name for the Rio Grande.

In a world economy increasingly conscious of tourism dollars, it is not surprising that travel television shows, travel cassettes, travel books, travel magazines and travel newspaper stories are big business all over the world. In her book *Six Myths of Our Time*, English writer Marina Warner details how a British newspaper, *The Independent on Sunday*, carried an article on New Guinea in the travel section. Offering the reader some grand excitement, the author of the article wrote, "but it isn't long since some of the missionaries were eaten." Warner points out that there were no specific cases of missionaries being eaten in New Guinea, but that stories about cannibalism had been part of the folklore of the region since it had first been explored by Europeans in the 16th and 17th centuries. In a book based on a series of British Broadcasting Corporation lectures, Warner focuses on how universal myths are perpetuated in movies, books, radio and paintings. The reference to cannibalism as a mythic motif is the only one in which she describes a newspaper circulating myth.

To conclude, I want to make one final point about the newspaper use of folk materials. Over the years, newspapers large and small have printed verse and poems on occasions ranging from the commemoration of an historical event, to the celebrations of a holiday, to the death of a local dignitary or ordinary citizen. These verses and poems, some anonymous, some authored by famous and not-so-famous writers, have functioned in the traditional lives of communities in a variety of ways.

In the 1950s, the late folklorist T. M. Pearce wrote and spoke about folk poetry in northern New Mexico. In a 1953 article in

Western Folklore, he defined the folk poet and mentioned certain writings by folk poets called "versos" which would later in the decade be identified by other writers as "in memoriam" poems published in New Mexican, Spanish-language newspapers, and in which a recently-deceased person is remembered. The poems are traditional in form, are often delivered in clichés, and are usually written by a relative or friend for the purpose of printing them in the newspaper.

Although I do not recall specific examples, I do remember having seen poems published in *The Dallas Time Herald* when I was a kid delivering the *Herald* to homes in my neighborhood in Oak Cliff. I am not sure if the poems were original and written on occasion or if they were familiar poems copied from other sources. In addition, I have vague recollections of having seen poems published in other sections of small town newspapers over the years. I do remember having seen patriotic poems published on July 4th or other U. S. holidays but do not recall the origin of those poems.

Just about every week my hometown paper carries a birthday greeting from a loved one or relative that includes some lines of rhyming verse. They are usually short, perhaps only two or four lines long. The most common one goes above or below an old photograph and reads, "Lordy, lordy, Look who's forty" or something like that. These birthday verses have been regular features in southeast New Mexico for many years and are similar to the congratulations announcements published for such things as graduation from high school or college.

I like T. M. Pearce's definition of a folk poet. In a 1953 article in *Western Folklore,* and later in Jan Brunvand's popular 1998 folklore textbook, Pearce wrote that the folk poet writes (1) of community events, (2) of individuals when their actions reflect community sentiment, (3) in traditional verse forms, (4) while emphasizing group feelings and thoughts, and (5) while suppressing his or her own personality.

I am including in this book of column pieces and news stories several poems written by Jean Granberry Schnitz of Boerne, Texas, who started writing poems for *The Kingsville-Bishop News* back in 1969 and has published many poems in that newspaper over the years. They are good examples of the kind of poetry Pearce described. Jean says she started writing her "Poet's Corner" when the editor Jake Trussell asked her to, and that her subjects have been whatever's happening in the community. She says no big city paper would ever publish her poems, but people in small towns are interested in the subjects of her poems—what the people are doing and saying during a particular period of time.

The idea for this collection of articles came from the 1998 annual meeting of the Texas Folklore Society in Sherman, Texas. At that gathering, twenty or thirty hands went up when members were asked how many had written for newspapers, and a considerable number of them showed interest in contributing to a book-length collection of writings that had something to do with Texas folklore and had been published in a newspaper.

The following writings are a sampling of Texas traditional life in the last half of the 20th century as seen through the eyes of some very diverse Texas writers. These full-time and part-time journalists have worked many years for large and small newspapers, ranging from far West Texas to deep East Texas, from the Panhandle to the Valley. Their subjects reflect the writers' own interests, but they reflect also the interests of the people in their communities. Their subjects are what the folk are doing and saying. Their subjects are the traditions, customs, and practices of the people in communities as diverse as the state is wide. Their subjects are the folklore of Texas.

A Legend Runs Through It

Bryan Woolley

The Dallas Morning News
June 28, 1998

ALONG THE PECOS RIVER, Texas—In Zane Grey's classic novel *West of the Pecos*, young pioneer heroine Terrill Lambeth gets her first look at the river and cries: "Oh, Dad! Take me back! This dreadful Pecos can never be home!"

"The place was desolate, gray and lonely," Grey writes, "an utter solitude, uninhabited even by beasts of the hills or fowls of the air."

But, plucky lass that she is, Terrill stays. The desolate Pecos becomes her home, where she lives happily ever after with a heroic cowboy whose name is . . . Pecos.

Writers of Western novels and makers of Western movies have always liked the name. "Pecos" sounds cowboy. Texan. And geography and history have made the river a worthy setting for tales of frontier valor and desperation.

The Spanish conquistadors, who saw the Pecos and its blistering Chihuahuan Desert in the 16th century, named the region *el despoblado*, the uninhabited place. Three hundred years later, pioneer cattleman Charles Goodnight cursed it as "the graveyard of the Cowman's hopes," and buffalo hunters claimed that when a bad man dies, his soul goes either to hell or the Pecos.

Despite its rigors, people have found reason to live along its banks. And the lives of its inhabitants—the Comanches, Kiowas and Apaches, the Mexican bandits, Texas Rangers, soldiers and stagecoach drivers, the cattlemen and cowboys, rustlers and nesters, the holdup men and treasure hunters, the women driven insane by loneliness and the incessant wind— have matched the toughness of their land and made their terrible stream the mythic river of the mythic West.

You wouldn't think it from seeing the Pecos now. For several decades, dams and irrigation farming have reduced it to a vestige of its frontier self, a mere trickle in places, no longer a killer of men and destroyer of dreams. Truckers and travelers crossing its bridges barely notice it.

"It's hard to believe it's the same stream," says Patrick Dearen of Midland, who has written four books about the Pecos. "Now it's shallow, it's smothered in salt cedars, it's polluted with oil. It's hardly a river anymore. You have to look deep to find the sweat and blood of the cowhands and immigrants and pioneers who saw in it a challenging obstacle."

Living along the Pecos still requires a certain strength, stamina and a sense of humor. If, they say, Texas ain't for amateurs, the Pecos is strictly for the hardiest professionals. Even for them, unless they were born there, life on the river is an acquired taste.

When Elgin "Punk" Jones, a cowboy turned oil-field worker, moved his wife Mary Belle and their babies to the east bank of the river forty-five years ago, she saw it as Terrill Lambeth did:

"I looked all around and said, 'My God, Punk, how long are we going to stay here?' And he said, 'Just till we get enough money to get somewhere else.'"

"I cried for three years. The wind and the dust would blow, and I would mop, and I would cry.

Pecos River near Mentone, Texas

"Well, we're still here. I got used to the quiet and the solitude. Now I couldn't imagine living anywhere else."

The Pecos begins as a clear mountain stream in the Sangre de Cristo Mountains northeast of Santa Fe, New Mexico. Trout live in its cold waters there.

As it flows southward toward its rendezvous with the Rio Grande 900 miles away, it nourishes the fields of Hispanic villages and Indian pueblos and the cattle of Anglo ranchers, good water in a thirsty land.

Then just above the Texas border, it begins to change. Gradually it loses its rocky bottom and flows instead through a soft adobe soil laden with alkali.

By the time it crosses into Texas for the second half of its journey, it has left behind all its mountains and coolness and sweetness and has entered a flat, hellish desert of mesquite and greasewood. Buzzards soar above the flat, torrid land. Dust devils dance across the plain like small, brown tornadoes. Oil well pump jacks dot the landscape, many of them leaking. Quicksand forms below the river's banks, and its water turns too salty for man or beast to drink.

A century and more ago, when the Anglos arrived to stay, the desolate Pecos was a place of cattle stampedes, Indian massacres, robberies, ghosts, lethal thirst and madness. Its name became a verb: to "Pecos" a man was to murder him and throw his body into the river.

"In those days, the Pecos was a very swift, turbulent stream with extremely steep banks and lots of quicksand," says Mr. Dearen. "Between the New Mexico line and the Rio Grande there was only a handful of places where you could cross it safely."

The first to cross it regularly were the Comanches, on their journeys from the High Plains to plunder the ranches and villages of northern Mexico.

In the early 1850s, immigrants crossed it to search for wealth in the California gold fields. So did Indian-fighting soldiers, marching to their West Texas forts, and stagecoaches carrying passengers and the mail from San Antonio to San Diego.

The river was a major hazard for them all. Along the seventy-nine-mile stretch of waterless desert between the middle Concho River and the Pecos, many died before they even reached its banks. One immigrant party drank the blood of its livestock to survive.

In 1866, Charles Goodnight and Oliver Loving drove a herd of longhorns from near San Angelo, Texas, to Fort Sumner, New Mexico, opening the Goodnight-Loving Trail. They lost 100 head to stampede and quicksand at Horsehead Crossing on the Pecos. But over the next decade they drove 250,000 cattle across the river, expanded the range of the longhorn as far north as Montana, and provided the inspiration for Larry McMurtry's epic, *Lonesome Dove*.

"In their day, the river was 50 to 100 feet wide," says Mr. Dearen. "During floods it spread to a mile. When the water receded, it left lakes of alkali water, a brine deadly to cattle. One early traveler said that at Horsehead Crossing you could step from one steer carcass to another for a square mile without touching the ground."

Over time, stories of hardships on the Pecos got enlarged into legends and tall tales. Rumor had it that beleaguered Spaniards had buried treasure in the desert, and that ghosts of massacred immigrants roamed the sand dunes near Monahans. A bigger-than-life cowboy called Pecos Bill became a nationally popular hero. As an infant, it was said, Bill fell out of his family's wagon as it was crossing the Pecos. He was reared by coyotes, fed his horse barbed wire, rode tornadoes and used a prickly pear pad for a napkin.

Those who popularized the tales claimed Bill was an authentic folk hero invented by cowboys swapping yarns around their campfires. But Paul Patterson, an eighty-nine-year-old cowboy, teacher and poet who has lived along the river most of his life, doesn't think so.

"Cowboys never thought much of Pecos Bill, because he could do anything without putting a strain on himself," he says. "That doesn't ring true with people in this country. You can't do anything here without straining yourself. Pecos Bill was a fabrication. Some writer made him up."

Yet libraries and bookstores still offer children's books, music CDs and video cartoons, written by authors and songwriters in Connecticut and California, celebrating Bill's exploits.

Early in this century, as the frontier was fading, the inhabitants of the Pecos became models for the heroes and heroines of Zane Grey and other writers of Western pulp magazine stories and novels. A few years later, Hollywood discovered the Pecos and cranked out such B movies as *The Pecos Kid* (Fred Kohler Jr., 1935), *King of the Pecos* (John Wayne, 1936), *The Stranger From Pecos* (Johnny Mack Brown, 1940) and *Robin Hood of the Pecos* (Roy Rogers, 1941).

Of course, none of them had anything to do with the real Pecos.

"The Pecos River holds a fascination for people," says Mr. Patterson, "unless they have to stop and camp and drink the water."

Skeet Jones, a son of Punk and Mary Belle, claims that after a coyote drinks Pecos River water, he immediately licks his behind to get the bad taste out of his mouth.

"It's just terrible," says Mr. Patterson. "It sears up your taste buds. One time when I was working on a ranch between where Rankin and Iraan are now, I broke the water jug. After a while, the fellow I was working with said, 'I just got to have some water. I can't do without it any longer.' He took two or three swigs of the Pecos, and he could do without water from then on."

Paul Patterson, Pecos

Mr. Patterson now lives in the city of Pecos, a few miles west of the river. At some 12,000 population, it's the largest Texas town along the stream. Pecos was the site of the world's first rodeo in 1883, an event still repeated every Fourth of July. In the hot, fertile fields that surround the town grow the world's juiciest, sweetest cantaloupes. In a small park near the center of town, gunfighter Clay Allison (1840–1887) lies buried.

Mr. Allison didn't die the Western gunman's traditional death. He was driving a wagon load of supplies from Pecos back to his ranch one day after lingering too long in a saloon. He fell off the wagon, and a wheel rolled over his head. "Gentleman and Gunfighter," his wooden grave marker says. "R.I.P."

To Mr. Patterson, such people are far more interesting than the superhuman characters that Hollywood and the novelists invented.

"Take Gid Redding," he says. "When I was a young cowboy, I batched a winter with old Gid. He was a top hand, and he could take the snakes out of the meanest bronc. I thought the world of Gid Redding.

"Well, old Gid, he became the last horseback bank robber in the United States. He robbed the banks at Hatch and Santa Rosa, New Mexico. They say old Gid had seven lawyers at his trial but did all the talking himself."

In 1931, not long after his winter with Gid Redding, Mr. Patterson—who cowboyed "four full years, seven full summers and a lot of weekends"—took the $22 his boss owed him and hightailed it to Alpine, where he enrolled in Sul Ross State Teachers College.

"What gave me a burning yearning for learning," he says, "was a big old gray horse that jobbed my head into the hard side of a hill. When I came to, I was wanting to do something else."

To finance his education, Mr. Patterson worked in a boardinghouse fourteen hours a day, cooking, slopping hogs and cleaning rooms. "I was envious of old Gid," he says, "up there in New Mexico, robbing banks, doing what he wanted to do, and doing it horseback."

For the rest of his working life, Mr. Patterson taught journalism, Spanish, history and civics in the Trans-Pecos towns of Marfa, Sanderson, Crane and Sierra Blanca, sometimes cowboying summers and weekends. "I was sort of a miscellaneous man," he says.

In Crane, one of his students was Elmer Kelton, now one of the best living practitioners of the Western novel. In Sanderson, Mr. Patterson courted and married another young teacher, who had grown up in the East Texas Piney Woods.

"When we moved to the Pecos country, she cried for two days and nights," Mr. Patterson says. "It was thirty miles between towns and farther than that between trees. But she learned to love it."

The origin of the word "Pecos," he says, is unknown. He thinks it may come from the Spanish *pecoso,* which means "freckled." "I figure the old Spaniards must have seen the sun glinting off the water and were reminded of freckles," he says.

He pauses, trying to remember. "Sometimes my train of thought derails," he says, "and I never catch the next one out."

Then he says: "You know, in the old days, when the men were off working cattle, a lot of women would be left by themselves for long periods. Some of them would lose touch with reality and lose their minds. Some of them were too crazy to know daylight from dark."

Lloyd Goodrich, Loving County

Lloyd Goodrich, a bachelor, lives on the land his grandfather homesteaded in 1906, and in the same weathered frame house. Sometimes he raises alfalfa in a field across the road.

His farm is near Mentone, around a bend in the road from Mary Belle and Punk Jones. Mentone is the only town in Loving County. About twenty people reside there. About 100 live in the entire county. That averages out to seven square miles per person, which makes Loving the most sparsely populated county in the lower forty-eight states.

"There's not much in Mentone now except the courthouse," Mr. Goodrich says. "You never know whether the damned cafe is going to be open or not since Newt Keene died. I don't even know who has it now. I go to Mentone maybe twice a week to get the mail, and that's about it any more. I don't circulate much. Hell, there's nobody to circulate *with!*"

Loving County lacks more than people. There's no school and no church. There's no cemetery. The last person laid to rest in the county was a cowboy who was dragged to death by his horse in 1929. He was buried on the lone prairie. Loving County's dead go to Kermit and Pecos for burial now.

There are 400 oil leases, which make Loving a wealthy county, but drinking water must be trucked in. Like people all along the Pecos, Loving County residents talk a lot about water and the lack of it.

"Hell, no, it's not as dry as it was in the '50s," Mr. Goodrich is saying. "Who told you that? It's nowhere close. In 1956 it rained on September 9, and it didn't rain again for eighteen months. Not a goddamn drop. Now that was dry!"

The scarcity of water in the Pecos country inspired a sixteen-year court battle in which Texas charged New Mexico with taking more than its share from the river. In 1988, the U.S. Supreme Court agreed. It ordered New Mexico to pay $14 million in damages.

"The Texas attorney general's office took $200,000 off the top for legal fees," Mr. Goodrich says. "The rest is in Treasury accounts, and the interest on it is divided among the seven water districts in the Red Bluff Water Control District. They spend most of it on legal fees. Damned lawyers. They're worse than the salt cedars."

Salt cedar is a scrubby brush introduced to the Pecos many years ago. It was supposed to reduce soil erosion. Now the river banks are choked with it. The line of dusty green salt cedar that runs across the desert like a scar is how you tell where the river is. An acre of it sucks up a million gallons of water a year.

Red Bluff, built in the 1930s, is the only reservoir on the Pecos in Texas. It's just south of the New Mexico line. Mr. Goodrich and other farmers irrigate out of canals from the reservoir.

"Trouble is, Red Bluff has only been full one time," Mr. Goodrich says. "The problem with farming along this river is that we don't have a reliable water supply. You might have water for six or seven years, then you might not have any for two years running. The trick is, you've got to get big enough or be small enough. It's the guys in between that are hurting. I've been out here a long time. I've learned I don't have to be rich. All I have to do is survive."

Mr. Goodrich, who is fifty-eight, can recall a time of less mesquite on the land and fewer salt cedars along the river. "I remember what it used to be when there was a lot of farming going on. I remember the smell of green alfalfa fields. Some people older than me remember cottonwood trees along all the ditch banks, and the river running most of the summer."

Now he's all that remains. He's the only farmer left in Loving County.

The Girvin Social Club

The Girvin Social Club has a rusty sheet-iron roof and, inside, walls decorated with cow and sheep skulls, neon beer signs and old license plates. There's a pool table in the back room and a wood-burning stove in the front. The owner is Walter Bohanan. His customers are cowboys and a few welders who have been imported to install a boiler at a nearby West Texas Utilities power plant.

Near the bar, six or eight fly-swatters hang from a nail. Mr. Bohanan is using one, too. He explains the reason for so many:

"It's a game we play. You get a fly-swatter and sit down at a table with three or four other fellows. Whenever you see a fly, you swat it and rake it into your pile. When it's time for another round, the fellow with the fewest dead flies has to buy. Then you rake them off on the floor and start over.

"You have to watch some of these guys, though. When nobody's looking, they'll reach down and pick up some of the dead flies and put them back on the table."

The Girvin Social Club has been open since 1956. Mr. Bohanan, who also operates an oil pump and supply business near McCamey, took it over last January. More and more, he says, he conducts his other business from his table at the club. "This place," he says, "is an oasis in the middle of nowhere."

It's also all there is of Girvin, except the home of Burl and Frankie Pringle, out behind the club.

The Pringles, Girvin's only residents, raise goats. Twenty or thirty of them move about their pens, constantly in search of food. There's also a llama, a rooster, a friendly German shepherd named Fancy and another, smaller dog.

Fourteen people lived in Girvin when the Pringles moved there in 1984. "Then the oil fields slowed down and some of them had to pursue jobs elsewhere," Mr. Pringle says.

"The rest died off," Mrs. Pringle says.

South of Girvin, the land begins to change. The mesquite and greasewood are joined by juniper, yucca and cenizo. The flat desert gradually yields to rocky hills and mesas, the range of goats and sheep.

October 28, 1926, the fabled Yates Oil Field blew in, revealing that the barren rocks covered an ocean of oil. More than a billion barrels have been pumped out of the field since then, and it's still going strong.

Yates Oil Field, Iraan

Iraan, a little town kept prosperous by the Marathon Oil Company, which operates the Yates Field, was named for Ira and Ann Yates, owners of the land on which the discovery was made. The town has a small museum full of fossils and oil-field and ranching memorabilia. Edna Brooks, who is ninety-three, runs it.

She and her husband ranched for many years along the Pecos, she says. She tells visitors of cows stuck in quicksand, of horses swimming in the swift current, of floods rising thirty-six inches deep into her house, of her sister dying of a heart attack as a result. "It was just too much of a shock to her, seeing the river like that," she says.

"But I wouldn't take any of it back. I wouldn't change it. I'd go back and live it again the same way."

A few miles outside the town, Dickie Dell Ferro has turned her grandfather's beautiful old house on the Parker Ranch into a bed-and-breakfast.

When he settled the land in 1907, Oliver Wendell Parker lived in a two-room cabin. When the Yates Field came in, he leased his land for drilling and built the big two-story house with the red tile roof. Ten years ago, his ranch was divided among his heirs, and Ms. Ferro got the part with the house on it. She runs a few cattle and has four rooms to let, and a rental house where a writer now lives, working on a novel.

In the fall, hunters come for the white-tail deer, which live on the flats, and the mule deer, which live in the hills. Noises of orioles, cardinals, tanagers, wrens, warblers, flycatchers, humming-birds and wild turkeys sing a chaotic chorus in the yard shrubbery and the brush beyond. Near the old wooden windmill in the pasture, buzzards hunch over a dead javelina.

"Peace and quiet we've got, which in the world today is about the rarest thing there is," says the writer, Meredith Rolley.

"I've lived in Odessa, Mexico, Wichita Falls, Lubbock and San Angelo, but this was always home to me," says Ms. Ferro. "I never liked anyplace except here. This is where I always wanted to be."

A River's End

Toward its end, the Pecos widens and flows between majestic limestone cliffs several hundred feet high, looking again like a real river. It passes under the High Bridge on U.S. 90, which replaced a lower bridge wiped out by the flood of 1954, when the river rose to ninety-six feet.

It flows by Langtry (population about twenty), where Judge Roy Bean ruled as "the law west of the Pecos." Strangers from the East would step off trains there to drink beer at Judge Bean's Jersey Lily Saloon and buy a round for his pet bear, Bruno.

With a six-shooter and a seldom-consulted volume of the laws of Texas, Judge Bean brought an eccentric but somehow appropriate brand of justice to the wild and woolly Pecos of the 1880s and 1890s.

The woman at the Texas Travel Information Center near the old saloon says 80,000 people a year drop in to watch a video about the old man and pick up a road map.

Then the river moves on past Comstock, a village not quite so small, and finally loses itself in the Rio Grande and Lake Amistad.

Amistad Dam, built by the federal government in 1969, backed up the Pecos for eighteen miles and inundated hundreds of caves where the first human inhabitants of the region lived 3,000 to 4,000 years ago. On the walls of their shelters they painted beautiful and mysterious images of beasts and shamans, indecipherable records of their deeds or dreams.

Some 250 painted caves remain, but the humidity created by the lake eventually will erase them all.

At Seminole Canyon State Park, where a few of the shelters are open to visitors, Robert Slaton, an employee, is talking about water:

"We're due another flood," he says. "We had a flood in 1932. We had a flood in 1954. We had one in 1974. We haven't had one since. So we're due one. And we need it. We need something to break this drought. We're looking at five years of drought so far. Since 1992."

After living in their shelters for thousands of years, the Pecos River cave-dwellers left. Nobody knows where they went. Nobody knows why. Maybe they couldn't take it any more.

The Weeping Woman

=================================== **John O. West**

The Fort Worth Star-Telegram
June 5, 1984

Among Texas' most fascinating women is La Llorona, the Weeping Woman, the focus of a migratory legend to be found in many cultures.

Not a historical character like some heroes and heroines—say Davy Crockett or the Babe of the Alamo—nonetheless La Llorona is real to many people.

She fits a pattern—in her behavior, when and where she appears—and she fills a need, much like defeated Southerners needed a don't-fence-me-in-model like Jesse James.

The Weeping Woman teaches a lesson—thou shalt not fool around outside your social class—or provides a scarecrow to keep wayward children (or even erring husbands) on the straight and narrow.

Although the legend of Llorona travels from place to place, she often acquires local characteristics to make her even more horrible or, like the flame that attracts the moth, even more fascinating.

Like many other dwellers in the Southwest, La Llorona is not native-born. In fact, the weeping woman garbed in white who haunts particular places—especially water—is found in many parts of the world.

In Germany, for example, she appears in Cologne as *Die Weisse Frau*. She is the spirit of a peasant girl, led astray and deserted by a naughty young nobleman: in a mad rage she killed their child, stabbed the father to death with his own sword, and later hanged herself—but she comes back regularly to haunt the scene of the double murder, and woe betide anyone who speaks to her.

Another girl led astray was reported in the Philippines after World War II. In this case the girl, of Spanish heritage, became the prey of Japanese occupation troops and the mother of several children. After the liberation she wanted to return to her native village, but the children were evidence of her shame, so she killed them—then went mad and sought in vain for her babies.

These two stories, albeit far in scene from the Hispanic Southwest, contain most of the essential details of the La Llorona story. In both stories there is a cultural or racial difference between the lovers, the girl kills the offspring and madness results.

The typical Mexican relative of La Llorona follows much the same pattern: a Spanish nobleman and a low-born maiden fall in love and have children. When he goes to Spain on business, he's encouraged by his parents to marry an eligible lady of his own class. On his return to Mexico, he breaks the news to his mistress, who goes mad and drowns the children and kills herself. But her soul cannot rest. She must search for her children forever until she finds them. Here the element of water occurs—and the basic pattern of La Lorona in the Southwest is completed.

In the El Paso area stories of the woman in white are plentiful, especially among the Hispanic population of low economic status. Told by children, they are simply horror stories; told by parents, they become obedience tales intended to warn daughters, especially, against liaisons outside one's own social level.

The pickings are rich indeed. Witness the following, collected in the El Paso area:

> *One night my uncle and one of his friends were coming home from the cantina. They always took too much tequila, you know, and so it was pretty late. All at once they saw this lady, about a block away, walking toward the canal. She really had a good figure.*
>
> *Well, you know how guys are when they've had too much tequila—they get interested in the ladies. So they hurried to catch up, and they even called to her, but she didn't wait. She walked on down by the canal.*
>
> *Finally they were just a few yards away, and they called to her to wait. Slowly, she turned around—and she didn't have any face! She lifted up her hands toward them, and she had shiny claws, like tin! And she was coming toward them, like she was going to get them, you know!*
>
> *Well, they turned and ran, with the woman right behind them, 'til they got to a bright street light, where she disappeared. My uncle never went to the cantina after that—he didn't want to meet La Llorona again.*

A story collected locally by Norma Herrera, a student of folklore at the University of Texas at El Paso, has an interesting twist:

> *When she was born, she was a twin. She and her sister were so identical, that when they were baptized, the other one was baptized twice. La Llorona was never baptized. She married when she was nineteen and had a son and a daughter. But she did not love them, so she drowned them in a ditch. When she died and went before God, He punished her by having her cry and search throughout the world for her children until the day the world ends. Then she will be pardoned. They say that she appears where there are lakes and ditches, and her weeping and wailing can be heard.*

As has been noted, La Llorona is usually found near water. And often the location is related to the crime that condemned her, like the Wandering Jew, to wander the earth searching for peace. One little old lady told the author about La Llorona, linking her sorrowful deed of drowning her children with the 1925 flood of the Rio Grande, providing believability with the detail of date—as well as making available enough water to drown any number of children.

In an occasional story told on the border, the rejected lover, crazed by the way she has been treated by her mate, kills their children and serves them as a meal to their father and his new love. Medea stopped short of making dinner of them, but not so "The Wicked Stepmother" of our Southern mountains who made the little boy into "rabbit stew." And many stories have as their theme La Llorona's hatred of men, luring them to their deaths or driving them mad, much like Lilith of Hebrew tradition.

Bacil F. Kirtley finds reason to believe that although there are apparent connections between La Llorona and the Aztec goddess

Civacoatl, there is much more evidence of European origin for the basic story, with local variants occurring, as is common in oral transmission, wherever a similar sort of tragedy has reportedly taken place.

Along the Texas-Mexico border, where a blend of Hispanic and Indian culture has dominated the scene for most of the last four centuries, it would be quite unlikely not to find the same sort of blending and variety as elsewhere in this worldwide narrative. The Lilith strain was found (with an interesting twist) by Ray Green and Federico Aguilar, Jr., in the following:

> *La Llorona hated men, especially men who have two or more women. She appears to them dressed in a white robe and makes a pass. And when they follow her they are always found drowned, sometimes in the canal, but sometimes they will be in the street. They always die with their eyes open like they were looking up at something and couldn't stop.*

They also found that the death of La Llorona's children is not always deliberate, although the result is somewhat standard:

> *There was a woman who had gone out into the fields one day to help her husband with the crop. She left her children unattended. When she came home that evening, she found all of her children dead. Somehow they had poisoned themselves. When she saw this, she went out of her mind and killed herself. Since a suicide cannot be admitted to heaven, the Llorona was condemned to wander the earth.*

William Campion found a lady of seventy-two who never forgot the lesson she learned many years ago:

As a young lady I often met Jose in the grove of trees near the river. Much kissing and loving took place but I was always careful to leave the area well before midnight. One night shortly before my engagement, time got away from me and I failed to leave before twelve. A cold chilling wind came up suddenly from the north with a furious intensity. A cat screamed, and a plaintive wailing sound came to my ears. It grew louder and louder until a blast of wind caused a white-robed figure to whisk past me. As the figure darted by, I saw that it had no face. I fell to my knees and sought God's help. Before long the wind stopped, and I could no longer hear the mournful cries. To this day, I have never returned to that cursed spot.

A youngster interviewed by Mary Lee Wight got her story straight from her mama:

My mother said to never go to the Rio Grande because if I do there will be this lady and her name will be La Llorona. My mother said if I went there the lady might drown me. She is always crying every time because she drowned her children. If you go she will drown you too.

In the dark of night, if one has been told often of La Llorona since early childhood, shapes and sounds bring back memories, and the goose bumps go up one's neck. La Llorona wants to get even with those who are happy; this is why men—the cause of her trouble—often are driven mad by the sight of her in the night.

What does La Llorona look like? Stories vary, but generally she looks beautiful—even enticing men closer—until one can see either the face of a horse or a blank, empty one. She dresses in long flowing robes—black or white—and her long, shiny fingernails are like knives by starlight.

Several years ago, people in one of the local *barrios* kept hearing La Llorona cry about eight at night, every night. They began to group together for comfort and protection—and whoever was making the sounds of La Llorona robbed the houses people had left in fear.

Such is the power of the tales of La Llorona.

Bois d'Arc Recollections

━━━━━━ Ernestine and Charles Linck

The Commerce Journal
September 24, 1997

O nce upon a time . . .

Well, it was when we left Phoenix on my ninth birthday, for the mortgaged eastern Kansas farm, that I first met what they called "hedge." Hedge had thorns. Hedge was used for fencing. Pioneer homesteaders had planted seeds for their boundary line fencing of quarter sections and other plots. Some called hedge balls "Osage Oranges," but inedible ones—not like the Phoenix ones.

Some hedge fences were kept trimmed down to about six feet and any empty spaces were latticed with the trimmed limbs to keep the cows and horses inside.

Trimming hedge was necessary. It was about the worst sort of job one could get, usually done with a "corn knife" (machete?). It took tough leather gloves and long sleeves to keep from getting scratched and scarred up.

Lots of earlier lazy louts had left off the trimming and let tree lines happen. Hedge trees can get about forty feet tall and bush out about the same on each side of the original fence, which means that some fifty to sixty feet of farm land on either side of the "fence" is barren.

Ultimately someone had to get busy and cut the trees down for fence posts and stove wood, piling the "brush" off into a ravine, where it made great rabbit housing for wintertime hunting. Tromping rabbits out after snows is fun.

Fence posts? Hedge logs five-, six-inches thick and eight feet long, buried two and one half to three feet in the ground and tamped in tight would support a three- or four-wire barbed wire (we never heard "barb war") fence that worked just as well as the old fashioned hedge fencing for keeping in the stock. Hedge posts last forever if sufficiently cured before setting. That wood gets hard as rock!

Firewood? If the non-post remnants were worked up for heating fuel for the pot-bellied stoves, the cutting needed to be done before total curing occurred. A cross-cut saw or a buzz saw could handle hedge before then, but it'd take a diamond-bitted buzz saw to cut through after curing! It'd make a buzz saw shrill in agony! Ever try cutting one of the "blocks" a Commerce house was set on? Hard stuff!

Cross-cut sawing? That's where I myself got started—on a cross-cut saw with my dad. There was an old pasture fence line that had grown into trees across the part that Dad wanted to clear out. This was before bull-dozers, so we used the cross-cut saw (also before chain saws) to fell the trees and hew out the posts, separating out the stove wood portions and the brush with axes. The stove wood poles were stacked awaiting the buzz saw operation and the brush was dragged to nearby gullies or other unusable spots.

Dad was fashioned a look-alike Swartzenegger with his 220 pounds of hard muscle which he had cultivated in Phoenix by stacking three bags of cement on his shoulder and climbing ladders with the load—effortlessly. Mexican hired hands looked on with mouths agape! At nine years of age, I was big, about 5'5", and carrying a fattish 145 pounds; enough to be on the other end

East Texas bois d'arcs. Photos courtesy of the *Commerce Journal*

of the cross-cut saw with Dad! He'd pull through rough; I'd pull through smooth. Even at that I thought I'd die!

Luckily when fall came around we three brothers had to go to school, so working hedge was only done on Saturday so far as we were involved. Actually I preferred trimming hedge to pulling one end of the cross-cut! Brother Bernard was built more like Dad; he liked the workout.

But during school days, our first evening job was to bring in the milk cows. There was this big Jersey bull. He'd spend lots of time under a lone hedge tree with a couple of his favorites who kept the flies away. They looked very stern when we approached to drive them into the milking shed. It was just the greatest luck that we kids discovered that Old Tom, a really ornery sort that even spooked Dad into carrying a pitchfork in the barnyard lots, could be intimidated by pitched hedge balls.

Bernard and I might have become big league baseball pitchers if we'd had enough time before snows covered our ammunition that fall!

Other uses for "hedge balls" were squirrel food. Squirrels loved those old rows of matured trees that lined most dirt roads or were boundaries between farms. Squirrels spent most of the winter scampering about hunting "hedge balls" that they could detect somehow under the snow. Feeding spots were clearly evident wherever there was a scattering of the wedge-shaped segments of the balls they discarded in the search for the seeds in the center. Those well cured and preserved seeds were about the best squirrel feed around, unless there were corn fields adjacent to the rows of trees.

Squirrels ensconced in their sticks-and-leaves nests in the hedge rows had real Mount Olympus ambrosia if there were corn fields nearby to vary their diets. Each squirrel could account for half an acre of corn if it weren't shucked by Thanksgiving.

Squirrels? We're supposed to be on the topic of hedge balls.

Squirrels just happen to be associated. Going on ten, I had permission to use a single-shot .22 to supply table food, a homesteaders' and Depression custom. Squirrel is good eating up in Kansas. I could easily find two or three fat ones along the tree lines. Winter time when there was snow, no wind, sleet, or stormy conditions, hunting squirrel was fun.

They'd hide behind a limb and continually creep opposite the hunter as he circled; it helped to have a good "ranch security" dog along. Springtime was the time for saving .22 bullets; a good mess of two or four squirrels could be acquired with just one or two bullets. Recent, fatter times' conservation laws have curtailed springtime hunting. Here in Texas, I doubt that anyone ever "proved-out" a homestead living on cottontails and squirrels. I'm not sure what the use of "hedge" was around here in white man times, except for foundation blocks under housing.

So far as I've noticed from the 1950s on, there don't seem to be any country dirt roads with rows of hedge trees one on each side as we used to have up in eastern Kansas. Those roads used to be horse-drawn grader "graded" regularly after a muddy spell. Along with erosion from rainstorms, they deepened year after year until finally the hedge trees began to slip and fall into the right-of-way, having to be dragged out somehow.

The age of bulldozers solved that problem. Bulldozers could have saved us lots of time and sweat. Modern dozers have pushed all the roadside hedge tree rows off into gullies and ravines (tractor farming caused lots of gullies in eastern Kansas). The banks have been sloped off and the roadbed graveled with crushed rock in the old township roads I used to know.

One has to look far and long to find a hedge ball up there these days; that's not the case down here in Texas, where historians say the original seed was harvested for use up there. Commerce may have thrived on the hedge seed commerce.

Ernestine's observations are that we "don't have to look long and hard for hedge balls around our house, what with seven healthy bois d'arcs in our back yard.

"They're trash trees, you know. My mother said so. Tacky. They have no place in elegant landscape design. The 'horse apples' (that's what we Texans call them, but don't use that appellation around an Easterner—I can't tell you why in print) are less than decorative.

"One year, though, Frances Hyatt and Shirley Erb decorated one of the trees down on Main Street close to Dick Latson's place with the balls for the Bois d'Arc Bash. It was a sight to behold!

"There are negatives, however. The other morning I strolled about the yard quite early to view the ravages of the Texas sun on bedding plants. And—Oops! Whoa! Ouch!—There I go again!—slipped on a squishy apple, went for a roll, landed on my you-know-what!

"Be wary, I admonished myself; those apples are out to get you!

"Thus it is, you, dear husband, have tried to placate my injured feelings about trash trees by running wisteria up a couple of them, a rose up another and a honeysuckle up a fourth. Or is that a trumpet vine? Yes, your plantlings make a fairly satisfactory cam-ouflage.

"But what can you do about the unpleasantness of being rudely awakened in the middle of the night by squirrels playing ball with the apples? In the attic? On the roof? Wherever!

"There's no use trying to sleep until the squirrels call time out. Preacher Enoch next door had problems with them, too; squirrels snitched silk neckties from his closet and used them for soft nests up under the rafters!

"I saw some kids playing ball in the street one day with the apples. What a mess the apples made! What the use of them can be is hard for me to see. Maybe mulch?

"I've watched you, dear husband, while you mow, stop to

pick up the squirrels' half-eaten apples and throw them into the free-form cactus bed.

"Neil Sperry has yet to recommend horse apples for mulch, but that cactus oval has become a beautiful sight. I counted, today, eleven of God's candlesticks ready to burst into bloom at one time—an unusual fall show. And lantana, daylillies, obedience plants, sufficient tunas on the prickly pear to make jelly. Three mesquite trees reaching for the heavens, a redbud, Carolina jasmine, a thriving native youpon. It is a circular island of beauty and a bountiful Garden of Eden.

"Someone said the apples would keep roaches away. We don't have roaches, but once, just to be safe, I put some on the lower shelf of the pantry cupboard. The things rotted! What a mess!

"Another said the tree's root made good dye for my homespun wool. I dug up and cut some of the strange, bright yellow root (roots of trees are supposed to be dark like the good earth, aren't they?). I boiled the root; I dyed my yarn. It turned out a dingy, dirty yellow, rather bilious looking. I don't need it. Kool-Aid is a much more satisfactory dye.

"The other day just as I stepped off the porch, an apple came rolling down the slope of the roof, headed for my head. Luckily I heard it roll and ducked. I looked up. There sat a squirrel, arrogantly, looking down on me. You'll never convince me that squirrel hadn't thrown the apple at me purposely!

"Yes, I do appreciate the shade those trees afford us on these hot, hot summer days. And now that we are committed to growing native plants in our yard, I can even be proud of them. But I still must remind myself those 'oranges' are deadly if I step on one and roll. Or if one falls out of the tree on my head. Or an unfriendly squirrel targets me. Beware!"

Prescriptions for Ailments Did Not Always Find a Cure

Joyce Gibson Roach

The Fort Worth Star-Telegram
October 6, 1996

Sickness, disease and accidents took their toll on those coming West. Statistics indicate that one-fourth to one-half—depending on conditions—died.

That is not to say that there were no medicines or homeopathic remedies for ailments, conditions and diseases.

Take ague: intermittent fever, chills, aching but not necessarily the flu. Today, it might be called a viral infection, or cold.

Or catarrh: irritated and inflamed respiratory tract from sinuses to lungs. Sounds like allergy to me, but then it could have been a viral infection, or a cold. Did I mention coughing and runny nose? Oh, yes, runny nose.

Or erysipelas, brought on by a specific streptococcus causing a contagious skin disease accompanied by fever.

Ague and catarrh were more likely to occur, or at least be worse, during winter.

Erysipelas could occur any time, but was considered epidemic during the Civil War. Not only was it passed from soldier to soldier, but to all the folks back home when a man returned.

Add stomach disorders and you have a list of four of the most common troubles—as in "I've got lung trouble . . . stomach trouble . . . skin trouble."

William A. Lopp, that venerable pioneer of Northeast Tarrant County who was a master farmer and chiseled excellent gravestones, was also a fine "folk physician."

His treatment for "Errispilis," as he spelled it, was as follows, also with Lopp's spelling and punctuation: "Two gram doses of Sugar lead in lard spoonfull at a time. grees well. reduce the Sistom with purgative medison. continue till cured."

General folk remedies added a salve made from white lead mixed with linseed oil, and soaking a cloth with muriate of ammonia to spread over the affected skin.

I'm guessing that the ammonia treatment burned so that you reached for grease of any kind.

Pokeberry roots made a good bath for rashes and itching, although no cure was claimed.

Fevers might be reduced with a dose of quinine and rhubarb.

Coughing might be helped with equal parts of honey and castor oil with a little alum. Or a quart of elixir composed of table salt and pure corn whiskey. Add pills made of ginger, pine tar, sugar, the yellow of an egg and a little flour.

Teas made from mullein or horehound—both wild plants—turpentine and sugar or honey and whiskey were effective.

Poultices helped coughing or aching. One recipe recommended quinine and grease rubbed on the chest.

Another suggested two parts crushed mustard seed to twelve parts of flour placed in a flour sack, heated and put on the chest.

A syrup made from milkweed root, honey and pine tar helped wheezing and lung trouble of almost any kind.

Some medicines grew or were brought to grow in the Cross Timbers by settlers.

Thomas Jefferson Thompson, who fought with Sam Houston in 1836 and returned in 1860 to claim land on Wilson's Branch near the Jellico settlement west of Grapevine for his service, brought along calamus roots, a folk cure for dyspepsia and colic.

Two other plants valued for their medicinal value were redroot and stillingia, but there were many more.

Folk remedies were passed along from one family to another, but frontier physicians generally offered the same or similar information.

By 1896, medicines of all kinds were available from the *Sears and Roebuck Catalogue.*

Under "Our Homeopathic Remedies," numbers rather than names of medicines were provided.

For example, No. 8R253 cured "catarrh, influenza and a cold in the head." No. 8R247 took care of "fever and ague, intermittent fever, malaria, etc."

Cost for the cures was fifteen cents a bottle. A medicine case and instruction sheet were free. Postage was two cents a bottle.

Specialty medicines were extra. The "Twenty-Minute Cold Cure" was seventeen cents.

All were designed to comfort and relieve. A more modern society declared that few homeopathic remedies cured anything.

Some of today's practitioners, a few doctors among them, say differently.

If you feel a touch of ague or catarrh coming on, you might reach for a sip of something with roots and leaves in it.

For that rash, keep the axle grease handy.

Endure an uneasy stomach. The cure is worse than the ailment.

Dyin' Easy and Several Other Ways of Crossing Over and Departing This Life

The Fort Worth Star-Telegram
August 25, 1996

The present generation does nearly everything well—and fast.

At death, dying and funerals, they do poorly and admit it.

Frontier folk lived a hard life, learned the savage art of survival, knew how to make do, get by and do without—and slowly.

They accepted the hard facts of dying as demonstration of Old Testament wisdom, "To everything there is a season, a time to be born and a time to die."

Although death and burial customs of the past are criticized as over-emotional, archaic, unsophisticated exercises by a folk society, pioneers knew the unwritten rituals, either prescribed by their cultures or simply of the heart, to get them through.

Their strange ways are worth retelling.

Rarely was someone dead referred to as "the deceased" or was death called "dying."

Rather, it was "departing this life," "crossing the bar *or* the River Jordan," "leaving this world," "gone to Jesus *or* to the bosom of the Lord," "passing or flying away."

To my mind steeped in the old, old ways, the finest vocabulary of death is the African-American expression, "she passed."

Not "passed away." Simply, "passed," as in passed by us on the way to somewhere else; or crossed some boundary without stopping.

Gaines County Cemetery

La Puerta Cemetery, South Texas

When someone died, a doctor, if available, was summoned.

Likewise, a preacher or a priest.

After the passing, the news was carried horseback and afoot by word of mouth to the larger community.

Certain rituals, mostly a dead folk-art now, were female responsibilities.

Family and intimate friends prepared the body in the house—no mortuary or funeral home.

The practice was called "laying out."

But the corpse needs a name, or else my descriptions are cold and morbid, and death and dying were neither, a long time ago.

I will supply a name. The laying out of Sister Caroline. Old Caroline, a saint of the Lord, passed in the springtime. She was placed on the bed until a wooden box, built on the spot, was finished—a male obligation.

Work began on hand digging the grave and crafting a marker, also a man's work.

William A. Lopp, who came to Tarrant County in 1866, is credited with chiseling many of the sandstone markers in Mount Gilead cemetery. Other markers were wood crosses, either plain or intricately carved by Tejano mourners (Mexican-Texans).

Large rocks and piles of stones, known as cairns, sufficed.

The dark reddish soil of the Cross Timbers was hard to dig and often a bed of clay appeared some two feet below the surface. The hole was stark, but there was a remedy. Some of the men lined the grave with cedar branches. Chicken wire was used at a little later time, but the cedar smelled good.

Children and women gathered wildflowers and handed them down to two men to intertwine in the cedar boughs. The inside of the pit was soon covered in every hue. The honey bees began their work immediately—a blessing. When the house was made ready and food brought by neighbors and friends—no relatives or immediate family were expected to clean or cook regardless of the race or culture involved—the "sitting up" took place.

Caroline's remains, clothed in her best Sunday-go-to-meetin' dress, were placed on the bed, because the burying box was not completed.

Some kept vigil beside her through the night and up to the very moment she was carried to the church or graveside.

It was during the sitting up that comforting and mourning began.

Those present began to ask about the passing.

"Did she die alone?"

"No. No. I was with her, holding her hand at the very minute she crossed."

"How did she pass? Did she die easy?" Meaning, was the death without suffering and pain.

"Did she know she was gonna' die?"

Often the answer was yes. Signs were everywhere.

Old Caroline had, weeks earlier, mentioned that she saw her mother walking past the gate. Uncle Euley motioned to her.

Five of her six children waved and called her by name.

Jesus beckoned. Angels came and went.

"The pale horse and pale rider came for her at last."

Superstitions were reviewed and strange happenings recounted.

"What were her last words?"

And then the stories about dear, sweet, ol' Caroline began.

"I remember the time . . ."

All through the night the litany of her life unfolded, decorating, enshrining and redefining her for those who began to mourn with loud crying.

"She was a good somebody."

"She stood straight up in a tumbled down world."

"She was too good to keep living in this sinful time."

The cycle, not yet complete, continues with the music, humor and ceremony of burying Sister Caroline.

Musing on Distant, Faded Glories of the Days of Radio

===================================== **Robert J. Duncan**

The Fort Worth Star-Telegram
Friday, March 23, 1984

The original E. T. is, of course, Ernest Tubb, The Texas Trouba-
dour.

I remember hearing E. T. on the radio in the 1940s singing *I'm
Walking the Floor Over You*. I took Tubb's lyrics too literally. My
childish imagination leaped to the image of a man murdering his
sweetheart and stashing the corpse under a plank floor. I imagined
something along the lines of Edgar Allen Poe's "The Tell-Tale Heart."

Tubb, like Hank Williams and Bob Wills, was a big star of
what we now call country music. Radio did a lot to boost him and
country music. He had been married to—and divorced from—
one of our very distant relatives, and the family was convinced
that Tubb's mournful songs were inspired by the breakup. As he
made his fortune, *we* knew that he was really pining away for his
lost love.

I listened to the radio a lot in the 1940s—my first decade of
life. On Sundays, Daddy filled the house with gospel music from
the Stamps Quartet. They really harmonized with selections like
Have a Little Talk with Jesus and *Turn Your Radio On*, which, I
think, was their theme song.

Television "soaps" are the illegitimate offspring of the radio soap opera. There was Stella Dallas, who kept being disappointed by her wayward daughter and saying, "Oh, Lollie, Lollie, Lollie."

There was Lorenzo Jones, the amateur inventor, and for some strange reason I can still remember the introductory music to his program.

There was *Just Plain Bill*, *Portia Faces Life* and *Backstage Wife*, which asked the question, "Can a Long Island housewife find happiness with a successful Broadway playwright?"

Mom and I listened to them all. We didn't call them "soaps"; to us they were "plays." Once a day Jack Bailey crowned the little lady who could tell the most believable sob story and proclaimed her "Queen for a Day."

In the evenings we tuned in to Fibber McGee and his rattletrap closet, to Baby Snooks and to one of our favorites, the Great Gildersleeve. On the more serious side were *The Shadow*, *Inner Sanctum* (which we called "The Squeaking Door"), *The Thin Man* and *Mr. District Attorney*.

We sat there on the edges of our chairs like the three bears—large, medium and small—listening to fairy tales. We spent untold hours staring at the radio, imagining the settings and action.

We were innocents at home. The Vietnam War, herpes virus and terrorists who "take credit" for assassinations were still nightmares yet undreamed.

Daddy always wanted to pack up and take a vacation to California. I think he even "studied out" how much it would cost. Like Abraham Lincoln, he used the back of an envelope to outline his best-laid plans and jot down his calculations.

Groucho Marx was beckoning. As we sat glued to our chairs each night listening to Groucho's *You Bet Your Life* and other quiz shows, Daddy discovered that he knew the answers to most of the questions. He envisioned our making a mint off old Groucho, or somebody.

On one of the quiz shows (it may have been *Truth or Consequences*), someone wrote a big check on the rind of a watermelon and had a contestant pull the watermelon all the way across the country in a little red wagon and cash it in a New York bank. They allowed him two weeks to pull it off. Of course, he must have hitchhiked, even if that was against the rules. But remember, this was before the days of interstate highways.

We were not far removed in time from the dance marathons of the Great Depression, and radio contestants were subjected to what today would be termed cruel conditions.

I remember one program on which they locked a contestant in a room with no windows. They gave him food and drink, and a few items that seemed absurd, such as a phonograph and a single record. He was allowed no clock, watch or radio. The object was for him to ring a bell during the half-hour program a week later.

In other words, he had to guess the correct time, plus or minus fifteen minutes, after seven days of isolation, with no inkling of daylight and dark. Quite a trick.

Of course, the guy was pretty smart, and as intended, he seized upon the idea of playing the record over and over and keeping track of the number of times he played it. The length of the song, in minutes and seconds, was printed on the label.

I listened to that program and was pulling for him, but he didn't call in time. Missed it by about two minutes, as I recall. The poor guy had just about worn out both sides of the record, and he nearly went berserk trying to stay awake and listen to it.

Maybe that's what turned Daddy off on radio contests. He never mentioned our proposed pilgrimage again.

Mankind has made a lot of giant steps since then, though I'm not so sure they've all been forward. Who could have foreseen uncensored color cable TV and video cassette recorders to freeze and replay our slightest whim?

Nowadays, radio is just something our cars come equipped with. Talk about wireless—now we do it with mirrors, and without imagination.

No doubt about it, baby, we've all come a long way. Now we're a lot richer—and poorer.

Unknowingly, Security Guard Takes on KKK

== **Robert J. Duncan**

McKinney Courier-Gazette
Thursday, March 14, 1996

My friend Jay Crum was the potential victim of a "set up" nearly forty years ago, but he didn't realize it until I broke the news to him recently. That's when he found out that he had been the first line of defense against the threat of a masked mob on horseback.

Jay was attending the University of Texas—the real one, I mean: in Austin. In about 1956, he was working part-time for a security company. On Halloween night they had him guard the home of an elderly woman on Windsor Road.

They instructed Jay to stay up all night and keep watch for anything suspicious. He was not to go in the house; he was just to hang around in the yard and, of course, stay wide awake.

A few young trick-or-treaters came and went early that evening, but later, the night was quiet and Jay got pretty sleepy. From time to time Jay would notice the curtains in one of the upstairs rooms move, and he sensed that he was not the only one who was staying up all night.

Around three o'clock, the old lady called to him to make sure he hadn't dozed off. When he answered, she said, as an after-

55

thought, "I should have baked you some cookies." Jay was a growing boy. He wanted to tell her, "It's never too late."

At daylight, Jay's boss picked him up and paid him twenty dollars for the night's work. He mentioned then that Jay had been guarding the home of the first woman governor of Texas, Miriam "Ma" Ferguson.

A couple of months ago, I happened to mention something about Ma Ferguson's administra-

Jay Crum

tion to Jay. That's when he told me about the Halloween night in the mid-1950s when he stood guard at her home.

Recently, I was reading a new biography about Miriam Ferguson. When I got to almost the last page of the book, I sat bolt upright when I read:

"Yet there were some enemies that would forever be enemies. The Ku Klux Klan never forgave her for destroying their organizations in 1925, when she was governor. Although twenty-five years had passed, they planned a final act of revenge, choosing, suitably enough, Halloween night of 1950.

"The grim spectacle was witnessed by the Threlkeld twin girls (who lived across the street), standing on their front porch in the gypsy costumes their grandmother had made them for 'trick or treating.' Darkness had fallen, when, seemingly out of nowhere, dozens of hooded riders on horseback, in full KKK regalia, descended down Windsor Road toward Miriam's house, bearing torches. The riders set their torches to the autumn-dry trees bordering the Ferguson house and they quickly began to burn, illuminating the corner of Windsor and Enfield. The riders vanished as swiftly as they had arrived. Firefighters came from the station at 10th and Blanco and extinguished the flame."

Jay was astounded when I told him. He had not been prepared to face a faceless mob on horses that night.

Mrs. Ferguson was apparently afraid the mob would return on other Halloween nights, so she hired a night watchman and helped keep the vigil herself on that spooky night each year.

The biography, recently published by Eakin Press in Austin, is entitled *Miriam*. It was written by my friend Maisie Paulissen and Carl McQueary.

Four Musings on Bad Roosters

================= **Henry Wolff, Jr.**

The Victoria Advocate
February 24, 1987

Henpecked

•

Vincent Rippamonti, Jr., was showing me where he'd been henpecked one time.

Sort of between the eyes.

Said he was just a boy at the time and was gathering eggs when an old hen got upset at him for sticking his face in her nest, and she let him have it pretty good, sent him home to Mama with blood running down his nose and for years afterwards he carried a red mark where the chicken had beaked him.

Chickens can be mean when they want to be.

Think all of us who have ever had to gather eggs can attest to that, and I know what it is to be pecked by one myself. We had a few when I was a kid that I wouldn't even mess with, would wait until they left the nest and then I'd sneak in and get the eggs. Not that I was chicken, but it just seemed to me to be the easiest way to go about it at the time. I never was all that fond of gathering eggs anyway, and dealing with an irate old hen wasn't my idea of making it any more fun.

Roosters were something else again.

Used to stand and fight with them at times, unless one started to get the best of me and then I'd run, which might sound kind of sissy to anyone who has never encountered an upset rooster, but sometimes it just seemed like the best choice to me. I remember hitting one once with a rock and knocking him cuckoo, and that was really scary because if I'd killed him then I would have had to answer for it.

Now you may think I'm making light of all this, but roosters can be dangerous and even an old hen if she's mad enough. What brought about Rippamonti telling me about the hen pecking him was something Raymond Leita told me. Rippamonti lives out south of Victoria toward Guadalupe on Farm Road 2615, across from the old two-story barn that Herman Zeplin built years ago as a dance hall. It was first located nearer the Port Lavaca Highway, but later on was moved and was being used as a barn around 1930 when the Leita family lived there for a time, and it was at the old barn that Leita says he lost the sight of his right eye in a confrontation with a rooster. He was only a little over a year old at the time, but the rooster didn't take that into consideration.

Suppose when a rooster sizes up a kid, even at a year old, it looks like a fair fight to him, and roosters like to fight even when they don't have a reason, like the old hen had when Rippamonti was trying to take the eggs away from her. We were always being warned when I was a kid to watch out for the roosters, that they could put an eye out, but then we were warned about a lot of things that we didn't always pay a whole lot of attention to at the time. I did think about it at times, when being chased by one, but until Leita told me what had happened to him I'd never really thought about it ever actually happening to anyone. If I had, think I might have run a little faster.

Thrown that rock a little harder.

The Victoria Advocate
February 26, 1987

Game Rooster

•

Lois Reeves says they had a bad rooster in Bloomington once.

Reeves had read our bit earlier on how cantankerous chickens can be at times, and it reminded him of a rooster Skinny Livingston had told him about.

"He's got chickens with a little bit of game in them," he said, "and one day a chicken hawk swooped down and carried off one of his roosters, took it all the way down into the Guadalupe River bottom."

He said the hawk really thought he'd caught himself a good meal, until he landed with the rooster.

"That rooster gave him a whipping you wouldn't believe," Reeves says. "Then he made the hawk fly him back home."

That sounds like a barbershop story to me, but Reeves says that's the way Livingston said it happened, and that he wouldn't doubt his word hardly at all.

It does go to show how tough a chicken can be, and some of them, especially if they've got a little game in them, will fight almost anything and even themselves if they can figure out a way to do it. I've seen a rooster fight himself in a shiny hubcap before, and it was just an old white leghorn rooster that thought he was seeing another rooster, or maybe just didn't like the looks of himself. Now some roosters are born to fight, but I think the white leghorn was probably just being protective. Roosters are that way, and they like to show off anyway, so you can't always tell exactly what they've got on their mind.

I gather that Livingston's rooster just wanted to go home.

Reeves mentioned something else that I'd kind of forgotten about, because it's been a long time since I've been around chickens on a daily basis, and that's how sometimes an old hen will get to thinking that she's a rooster, even acting like one. Sometimes they will get where they'll even try to crow as best they can, and Reeves said his father would wring their heads off when they'd get that way, although he never explained exactly why. Would suppose he figured that a hen acting like a rooster wouldn't find time to lay many eggs.

There's sort of an unwritten law about such matters in regards to chickens, that when a hen won't lay she shouldn't eat, but should be eaten. If that chicken hawk had picked out an old hen it might not have gotten in near as much trouble as it did messing with that rooster.

Kind of makes me hungry for a baked hen, now that I think about it, and that's about the best way I know to eat chicken. Baked rooster isn't bad either, if you don't mind fighting with one over what you're going to eat. We used to have one of those wire hooks to catch chickens with, and trying to put that thing around a rooster's leg was sometimes more work than dinner was worth, but the good thing was that by the time you finally had him caught you were mad enough to chop his head off.

Then he'd still want to fight you.

The Victoria Advocate
March 6, 1987

Thinking Chicken
•

Been carrying a calendar around from the Hornung Hatchery on the dashboard of my car.

Might be why I've been thinking about chickens so much here lately. Monroe Marek of Cameron sent it by way of Joe Strauss of Shiner. I met Marek at a backyard gathering at the Strauss home during the Shiner Picnic last year, and got to asking him about the hatchery since for years I'd wanted to get one of their chicken calendars. Used to have just about any chicken you could think of on the calendar in color the way they really looked, and it's still in color except they don't offer near as many kinds of chickens as they used to. What they show on the calendar are English white leghorns, strain cross Layorcas, production reds, barred rocks, and Cornish X rocks.

The white leghorn rooster on the calendar looks like a real proud bird, and I'd like to have him out in the back yard to serenade me in the morning when the sun's coming up. I like to wake up to the sound of a rooster, and then go back to sleep again knowing everything is all right outside. Neighbor down the street used to have a few chickens, and I always liked to hear his rooster crowing. To me it's one of those pleasant sounds, like church bells in the distance, surf pounding on the beach, and gentle rain falling on a tin roof.

Our comments recently about how mean some roosters can get reminded Emma Kopecky of Port Lavaca of a rooster that her folks had when she was a girl in Louisiana. She says they lived on a sugar plantation where her dad worked in the mill, her mama cooked, and she washed the dishes. They also had some chickens, as practically everybody did back then. The old hens had got where they'd squat down every time somebody walked in the yard, and they got the rooster to see if they couldn't get them to thinking more about laying eggs. Mrs. Kopecky says she was heading across the yard to pick up a little duck when the rooster took offense and attacked her leg, first spurring her to the bone, then he jumped on her back.

"Seemed like it took Mama fifteen minutes to get him off," she says. "He was a big one."

She says later on he attacked her mother two or three times, and she put him in the gumbo pot.

I think chickens add a homey touch to a place, and there's still quite a few folks who have some, but nothing like it used to be when everybody on the farm had a flock of laying hens, and a lot of folks in town kept a few where they could. Doesn't take a lot of chickens to provide enough eggs for a family, and a pen of fryers can get you through a bunch of Sunday dinners.

Come to think of it, this is about the time of year to start thinking about getting baby chicks. Remember how we used to get them early sometimes when I was growing up, and then a cold front would blow through and we'd have to bring them in the house with us and put them in a box near the stove. Even when we used a brooder, we'd end up with some of them in the house for one reason or another, those who were too weak and couldn't take care of themselves and what not. Put them by the fire, and feed them a little dry oatmeal, and we'd have some of them beeping again in no time at all, sometimes all night long.

Until the rooster crowed.

The Victoria Advocate
July 28, 1987

Attack Rooster

•

Mrs. Don Lynch recalls how her son was once attacked by a rooster.

Nothing serious, just one of those little skirmishes that kids and roosters get into at times, like we mentioned a while back on the subject of how cantankerous roosters can be.

Think about everyone who has ever lived on a farm, back when we all had chickens, can recall at least one such incident. Little boys seemed especially adept at becoming involved in such barnyard altercations, and roosters are not beyond accepting anything that appears to be a challenge.

Mrs. Lynch says her son, Luke, who now lives in the Dallas area, was only three years old at the time and had on a pair of cowboy boots that he was quite proud of, and she figures he probably kicked at the rooster while trying to get it to play with him. At any rate, the rooster took offense, and before she broke it up the rooster had his wings wrapped around her son and the feathers were flying.

She didn't want her son to be scared and told him from then on when he got around the rooster to flash his cowboy belt buckle at him, and that would keep him at a distance. She said little Luke would do that every time he got near the rooster, sort of strut around with both hands on the buckle shining it at the feisty bird, and it seemed to work. The rooster probably just didn't know what to make of it; at any rate he left the boy alone.

Mrs. Lynch, now of Colorado, is the former Chris Gerlich, and says she was born in Breslau, near Hallettsville. Met her at the armadillo festival when the Shiner Hobo Band was playing, and she was particularly interested in the band since her cousin, Hubert Gerlich, is one of the musicians.

She said our column about cantankerous roosters just happened to remind her of Luke's experience.

I'm reminded of once when I was a kid and a rooster got after me, but I was a little older at the time and picked up a rock and threw it at him, which much to my surprise hit him where it hurt most—in the head. It knocked the rooster cuckoo for awhile and that scared me more than anything, because he was flopping around like I'd chopped his head off and I thought he was probably going to die and then I'd have to explain how come I'd killed him. Even though it was in self defense, I wasn't sure it would be an acceptable excuse, but luckily the rooster regained his composure after awhile and after that seemed to have a great deal more respect for me. If I'd known about the belt buckle, it might have saved me some worry there for a moment.

Thing about the belt buckle, I don't think you'd want to get close enough to let a rooster see himself in one, because next to other roosters and young boys there is nothing I know of that can upset a rooster more than seeing his own reflection. I base this bit of inconsequential knowledge not so much on scientific fact as on observation, because I have seen some awfully mad roosters looking at themselves, like the old rooster I previously mentioned that liked to get in a fight with himself anytime he walked by our car and saw his reflection in a hubcap.

Don't think he ever won one of those fights that I can recall. Might say he'd met his match.

The Ol' Red Rooster Learns a Hard Lesson

=========== Lora B. Garrison

Uvalde Leader-News
February 1, 1987

The following is a true story and I believe it happened the year Mama grew so many English peas that she sold fourteen bushels.

Everybody called Mama "Granny." All the grandchildren called her Granny, all the children called her Granny, all the in-laws called her Granny, all the neighbors called her Granny, friends called her Granny. Just everybody called her Granny.

She lived to be ninety-three years old. She passed away just a few years ago and she was Granny as long as she lived. She is still Granny.

Well, Granny always had the finest garden of anybody in the whole country. People would come from miles around to admire her fine garden. They would want to know, "How in the world do you have such a fine garden, Granny? Why, my corn is only about three foot high. How did you get this corn that's ten foot tall?" And all those things like that.

"Well," she says, "I just always planted it in the right signs of the moon." She hauled a lot of Red Flyer wagon-loads of manure from the cow lot, too, believe me, because I remember. I had to help do it.

When Granny first started to raise English peas she had read about some real special kind that would produce tremendous quantities. And she decided she had to have some of those seeds. I believe she paid $4.98 for a package of only fourteen seeds. Now that was a terrible price to pay during the Depression years for anything, much less only fourteen seeds.

But the garden being her pride and joy, and the source of almost everything we had to eat, she decided it would be worth it.

Of course it was a lot of trouble to get the seeds. You had to write down out of the seed catalogue and order them. Then when they would come in to the post office at Rio Frio, somebody would have to ride the horse five miles over to the post office to get 'um. It was hard to come by seeds; so you were very careful with them and you would save your seeds every year so then you would have a start for your garden the next year.

Well, this one particular year Granny got those real special pea seeds. When they came in she studied her calendar and she decided when the moon was just right, when she was going to get those peas planted.

Granny and Little Brother John went out to the garden, laid out the row and planted those real special pea seeds. They got them all laid out real nice, put those pea seeds in the row, covered them with dirt and watered them in.

Then they went up on the front porch (Papa always called it the gallery). We had big rocking chairs with wide arms up there on the porch and there was always a nice breeze coming out of the southeast. That's the only place Granny would ever sit down and rest. Usually she didn't just sit down there and do nothing. She had some beans to shell or some mending to do or something; she wasn't ever idle. She didn't let the children be idle either. Usually this was when we could beg a story out of her.

So Granny went up there to sit down for a little while to rest on the porch, and cool off a little bit. She looked back out there in the garden, and what do you suppose she saw?

Well, there was this great big ol' Rhode Island Red rooster out there going down that row, just a scratching up all her pea seeds and gobbling up all her fine pea seeds, and he had eaten every one of them.

Granny said, "I don't know what in the world I'm going to do, I planted all my pea seeds; and I was sure counting on that crop this year."

She said, "John, you go out there and catch that rooster, I want that rooster."

John told me he didn't know what she was going to do with that rooster, he thought maybe she was going to wring his neck and put him in a pot for supper. But he knew he better do what Granny told him.

So he went out there, got the dog and chased that rooster down. He got that rooster back in the corner of the garden, he and the dog, and they caught that rooster.

Well, he brought that rooster back in there to Granny. He walked through the gate carrying that rooster by the feet, its wings a-flapping. Granny came down off that porch and met him out there in the yard and she took that rooster by the feet and she walked back over there to the porch and she flung that rooster down there on the edge of that porch.

Granny reached in her apron pocket, pulled out her pocket knife, opened up her pocket knife and she cut that rooster's neck open.

Well, she reached inside that rooster's neck, she pulled out that rooster's craw, she cut that rooster's craw open, and then she started peeling out all her pea seeds. She got every one of them; peeled every one of those pea seeds out of there, all fourteen.

Granny reached back in her pocket again; and she pulled out a spool of thread and her needle, and she sewed that ol' rooster's craw back up. She put that rooster's craw back in him and then she sewed that rooster's neck back up.

She took that ol' rooster out there and throwed him out there in the pen with the hens and he just went on doing what a rooster is supposed to do. It didn't hurt him a bit. She couldn't have killed him; he was the only rooster she had on the place.

Well, Granny took those pea seeds and she went back out to the garden and she cleaned all her rows out and she planted those pea seeds again. She got them all watered back in there.

And what do you think that rooster did?

Sometimes when I tell this story, children will say, "He went right back out there and he dug those pea seeds up again!"

But I'll tell you what this rooster did. That rooster, he didn't go near that garden no more neither.

Well, Granny grew the finest crop of peas that year you ever did see. People just came from miles around to admire her fine garden. They said, "Granny, how did you grow such a fine crop of peas?"

And she smiled and said, "I just watched the signs and planted them in the moon, that's all I did."

Hallie Stillwell Will Live on in Memories

=== **Kent Biffle**

The Dallas Morning News
Sunday, August 24, 1997

ALPINE—More than 1,000 species of plants and more than 435 species of birds are found in the Big Bend. But there was only one Hallie Stillwell. She died last week.

"She left a big hole in my heart," said her grieving granddaughter Linda Perron of Alpine.

Hallie Stillwell was a dainty, poker playing rancher who once plugged a mountain lion between the eyes. She arrived in the Big Bend eighty-seven years ago in her family's covered wagon.

The grande dame of the greasewood had long planned a big 100th birthday bash, but congestive heart disease intervened. About 100 friends and kin attended her funeral in Alpine on Wednesday, just two months short of her centennial celebration.

"We'll go on with the party," her daughter Dadie Potter told me. "We'll hold it in the Brewster County Park, five miles south of Marathon, on the afternoon and evening of October 18.

"The public's invited, just as Hallie planned it."

Going on

Mrs. Potter said the family will go on running the Stillwell

Store and the Hallie Stillwell Hall of Fame Museum on the 15,000-acre Stillwell Ranch southeast of Marathon.

She had a house with a green lawn in Alpine, but she preferred to reside on the ranch, her gorgeously hostile desert domain.

In her old adobe ranch house years ago, I quizzed her about her impressive longevity.

Smoke?

"No."

Drink?

"No."

She winked.

"We have plenty to do out here without smoking and drinking."

Like what?

"Lying, stealing mostly," she said happily.

A tall, silvery haired monument to frontier fun, gallantry and gumption, she was—way back in Pancho Villa days—a schoolteacher in Presidio, where she packed a six-gun to ward off border-crossing raiders and drunken U. S. soldiers.

Unforgettable

She was an unforgettable presence. I know a sophisticated, big-city journalist (Mike Cox of Austin) who was so taken with her that he named his daughter Hallie.

She was the widow Stillwell for nearly half a century. Roy Stillwell was smitten in 1917. Courting her, he hired a fiddler and guitarist to serenade her bedroom window in Marathon. They sang and played *Listen to the Mockingbird*, an old song about a girl named Hallie:

"I am dreaming tonight of Hallie

Sweet Hallie, sweet Hallie . . ."

With four months of wooing, Roy Stillwell won her, wed her and moved her to his remote ranch house in a dagger flat twenty

Hallie Stillwell's Hall of
Fame, Big Bend

miles north of the Rio Grande. There they set up housekeeping with one house and four cowboys. Unstylishly, she wore pants and rode astraddle.

Her misadventures and accomplishments on the ranch before Roy Stillwell's death in a truck crash in 1948 are told in the first volume of her autobiography—*I'll Gather My Geese* (Texas A&M Press).

The book's title comes from her sassy reply to her father (Guy Crawford) when he called her teaching career in Presidio "a wild goose chase." She snapped: "Then I'll gather my geese."

Dadie Potter promises me that the second volume's still in the works. Her mother originally wanted to call it: "My Goose Is Cooked."

Truth to disclose, I think her goose is only half done.

A&M Press has set no publication date. Another granddaughter, Brenda Trudeau of Presidio, who helped write the first volume, has completed ten chapters. Her grandmother's memory began taking vacations during the interviewing.

The second volume needs doing because it will cover the widow's years as a justice of the peace in a precinct half the size of Connecticut in 6,200 square-mile Brewster County, a territory big enough to declare war and print its own money.

Moreover, volume two will record the Terlingua chili wars where for years Queen Hallie ruled in a crown of peppers.

Some liked it hot. And volume two introduces several: chili tycoon Homer Thomas Wilson (Wick) Fowler (1909–1972); *The Dallas Morning News* columnist Frank X. Tolbert (1912–1984); and a man who claimed to know more about chili than anyone, H. Allen Smith (1907–1976), who wrote a best seller, *Low Man on a Totem Pole*.

Brenda Trudeau showed me a fragment of her grandmother's recollection of the world's first chili cookoff in Terlingua three decades ago:

"Judges were picked. I was picked by H. Allen Smith. Floyd Schneider, vice president of the San Antonio Chamber of Commerce, was chosen by Wick Fowler—some say he was bribed by Fowler and paid well for his vote. The third judge was Dallas attorney David Witts.

"The day of the cookoff, the mud-slinging really increased. Frank Tolbert of Dallas had written several articles for *The Dallas Morning News* promoting the cookoff and Fowler's chili.

"Smith told me that he caught Fowler's goon putting grasshopper legs in the Smith chili. Fowler claimed that Smith's secret recipe called for carrots and beets in the chili. Smith called Fowler a Texas hippy. The contest rose to its expectations.

"When the judges tried the chili samples, I tasted first. I rolled the chili around on my tongue, coughed several times, and swallowed hard. I drank two glasses of water after trying Fowler's chili.

"I tried Smith's chili. It set my eyes to tearing and my nose to running. I savored the spices and tasted the flavor, although it was awfully hot. I voted for H. Allen Smith.

"Schneider cried a lot more than I did. He voted for Fowler.

"That left Witts, mayor of Terlingua, as the tie-breaker. He tasted both.

"He cried, teared, coughed, sputtered and spit. He couldn't handle the heat.

"He declared a moratorium due to his burns stating, 'It'll take a year for me to git back my taste buds. I can't vote. That stuff's just too hot.'

"And so it was. The first chili cook-off in Terlingua ended in a stalemate. There was no winner."

Ex-Sheriff's Tale is One for History Books

Kent Biffle

The Dallas Morning News
Sunday, October 11, 1998

Smile.

Nonagenarian Corbett Akins, longtime sheriff of Panola County, is recalling his Piney Woods boyhood for a bunch of teenage historians from Gary High School's *Loblolly* magazine:

"When I was a small boy, we'd kill our hogs in the fall and hang the meat in the smokehouse. Our job was to see that the hickory fire was burning in the smokehouse to dry the meat.

"We would take the fat part of the hog, chop it up, and place it in a pot to boil. After letting it cool, we'd dip the lard off. The part that was left was the cracklings.

"We put the cracklings in a tub and took it to the smokehouse. While they were warm, we would place them in jars.

"My brother, Horace, and I were looking after the smokehouse to make sure the fire kept burning. My mother left that afternoon to help a neighbor quilt. She told us not to let the fire go out. My papa had gone to Carthage to be on the jury. He had to ride thirteen miles on a mule.

"Horace and I got all the cracklings squeezed into the crackling jars. We had vented up the fire. We were sitting there, two little boys playing and having fun.

"I picked up this small, greasy churn that we'd had cracklings in. When he turned around, I put that churn over his head. I was not thinking about any trouble. Naturally, he reached up and tried to get the churn off his head, but he couldn't. After he worked a good while, I tried to get it off. I pulled on that churn until I gave out.

"We wrestled with it from about four P.M. until dark. When my mother came in, she wanted to know where Horace was. I told her he was in the smokehouse with a churn over his head.

"We led him in the house and sat him on a chair. Mother worked with him about an hour. She could not get it off.

"After she failed, she told me to prepare for supper. I went to eat supper. My brother couldn't eat because the churn was on his head.

"It was cold at bedtime, so we had a big fire a'goin' in the old fireplace. My bedstead was about six feet high. Horace would roll and tumble on the bed. He kept hitting that churn on the bed-stead, so that I couldn't sleep. It is a job to sleep with a fellow with a churn on his head.

"About two A.M. my daddy came in from Carthage off the jury. My mother told him the story, so Papa got Horace out of bed and sat him on a stool. Papa worked with Horace thirty or forty minutes. He had his head nearly pulled off.

"Finally Pap got tired. He made my mother go get the hammer from his toolbox. She says, 'Don't do that, that will kill him.' He says, 'Well, he's gonna die anyhow, so get me my hammer.'

"He hit it a few licks. The churn burst all to pieces. By that time Horace's ears were all swelled up as big as bananas. Blue and swollen.

"For several days his ears set up above the place where his ears should have been."

Corbett Akins and his father. Courtesy of *Loblolly*,
Gary High School

One of a brood of ten Akins kids, Horace survived his smash-
ing misadventure. And Corbett swept all his churning misdeeds
out of sight in order to win election as constable and then as
sheriff. He was sheriff from 1942 to 1952. He died nearly a decade
ago. I know him only through his memoirs recorded by *Loblolly*
staffers and historian Thad Sitton (*Texas High Sheriffs*). Tapes res-
urrect the old man's fighting-cock personality. I'll get back to him.

Gary High School's unique. How can a school with 115 students publish a readable, award-winning magazine twice a year?
Moreover, how can this be done at a school that can't even field a
football team?

The answer is Lincoln King. Teacher King, sixty-seven, dreamed up *Loblolly* twenty-five years ago. Kids sold subscriptions to pay for the first issue of the journal, named for a native East Texas pine. *Loblolly* has been self-supporting ever since. Proceeds pay for publishing costs and for a modest accumulation of editorial and photo equipment.

Sponsor King keeps a talented eye on things, but he insists that the kids do the work. He's never even bothered to learn to operate the two computers in the *Loblolly* office.

This week, *Loblolly* distributed a hardback collection of favorite articles and artwork published in its first quarter-century.

Titled *Loblolly Looks at Panola County*, the 250-page hardback is twenty dollars at The *Loblolly* Project, Gary High School, Box 189, Gary, Texas 75643. Yearly subscriptions to the magazine are eight dollars.

The twenty-fifth birthday book was edited by Cassie Downing, a sixteen-year-old junior, and Sierra McGarity, eighteen, now a computer science major at the University of Arkansas.

It's a big, good-looking book, a sampler of the magazine's down-home tips on subjects that range from infant care to mule care. There's folksay on homeboy Tex Ritter and road-dusty Bonnie and Clyde. And there are oral history interviews with the likes of Corbett Akins.

Named for long-ago heavyweight Gentleman Jim Corbett, Sheriff Akins revealed pugilistic secrets of his own: "I've had more fights than jaybirds had eggs, but I was always smart enough that when I was arguing with a man, I'd get close enough to get in the first lick, and it's the first lick that counts. First thing he knew, I had him on the ground. I'd either hit him with my billy or my pistol or my fist, but, anyway, he went down."

He told the kids he wrecked a couple of dozen moonshine distilleries in the woods not far from their high school. He told of seeing drowned possums and rats in the vats of mash. Care for a drink? Whooeeee.

"I wouldn't want to tell you how many men I've killed," said the lawman whose quick pistol once knocked down sparrows on the wing. He told the kids he'd been shot at eleven times, boasting that he knew of no other man who'd been shot between the eyes and lived to tell it:

"This fella came running out of the cafe and got off one shot. Lucky for me, I was turned just a little bit sideways and the bullet grazed the bridge of my rose, right between the eyes. Still got a scar. But, yes sir, you can bet I played Waxahachie on his rear end.

"I was mean as hell."

Brother Horace would have agreed.

Tales of a Rural School Teacher

Lou Rodenberger

The Fort Worth Star-Telegram
Monday, June 4, 1984

"Them ol' big boys run off that last teacher. Let me tell you, that was some story." So the storyteller begins.

Such a narration is traditional lore in the history of most Texas rural schools, though the schools themselves have long since closed. School trustees always related the latest circumstances of a teacher's hasty departure to the next hopefuls who wanted the job—sometimes with a touch of braggadocio and always with gusto.

These stories are part of the lore still remembered and passed on by the many gray-haired Texans who learned to read, write and figure in a country school.

I have heard these tales from my parents, Carl and Mabel Halsell, who taught more than forty years in the rural schools of Texas. The revered Texas folklorist, Mody Boatright, once designated family stories as vital contributions to folklore and called them "family sagas." Experiences in my family saga reflect those of most rural teachers in Texas from 1920 until 1950.

No dams controlled the ebb and flow of the meandering Brazos River in 1929 when my father drove down a narrow ominous road through a dark valley along the Keechi in Palo Pinto County to a two-teacher school called Lucille. The school unified the scattered community of ranchers, farmers and oil field pumpers about two miles east of the river.

My father had just learned that the burly principal would not be back the next year. Only weeks before several boys had "run him off" with a baseball bat.

A vicious, dismal spring sandstorm rocked my father's 1926 Chevy as he sat that evening in front of the dingy schoolhouse with the three trustees and made a deal. The leader, who lived across the Brazos, said discipline was all he was interested in.

"Hell," he said, "I lost a crop last year swimming the river to settle disputes between the teacher and the kids. What I want to know is can you handle them ol' big boys?"

My father, who never weighed more than 140 pounds, gave his stock reply. He would teach a month and if he wasn't handling the situation to their satisfaction, they wouldn't owe him a dime, and they could get another teacher.

Two of the trustees were convinced. They crawled out of the old Chevy, and with the wind whipping their clothing and the sand stinging their faces, the trustees hastily scrawled their signatures on the form contract my father had handy as they hunched in the dim light of the car's headlights. The salary they penciled in—$125 per month for eight months.

At Lucille—as at Romney, Kokomo, Okra, Cottonwood, Pultite— he stayed. He and my mother quickly gained the respect of their rough-edged students.

My father had learned the art of self-preservation as a runty kid in Hawley, still a West Texas frontier town in the early 1900s. Because of his size, he learned to use his head to stay out of dangerous situations. His knowledge of human nature yielded an elementary psychology that worked with school kids: Know your clientele, anticipate their next move, learn the value of bluffing and keep 'em busy.

(above) Romney School near Cisco, where Carl and Mabel met 1921–23

(left) Carl Halsell and Mabel Falls in 1922

(below) Romney students and two teachers, Carl and Mabel

Here is how my father says he learned the art of anticipating a mischief-maker's next move: "When I was a boy, my father gave me an orphan colt. When she grew up, I broke her to ride and work. When I was about fourteen, I rented six acres of land and planted it in peas, corn and melons.

"This mare had peculiar ways. She wasn't balky or mean, but she had a mind of her own. I tell this because I got one of the greatest lessons from her—study your subject and anticipate the next move. I watched her at work. When I knew she was going to stop and rest, I beat her to it and yelled, 'Whoa.'"

Early in his career, he put his theories to practice. Three simple rules governed the boys' activities while they were on the schoolground: No fighting, no cussing, and no tobacco chewing. His ability to identify with adolescent boys resolved one clandestine rebellion.

Here is his story:

"The boys' outdoor toilet was in the southeast corner of the schoolground, which was surrounded by a brushy woodland. About a hundred yards out in the brush there were a lot of big tree stumps. At the noon hour, after we had played basketball for about thirty minutes, I would take the ball and tell them they had about twenty minutes before I rang the bell for 'books.' They would always run the little boys back and not let them tag along. They worked it smart. They would dodge behind the toilet, crawl under the fence and make for the woods. One day after I caught onto what they were doing, I crawled over the fence away from them and slipped up on them. "Each one was seated on a stump with a big chaw of tobacco in his cheek. When I walked into their presence, it scared them so badly that one of them swallowed his tobacco. Those ol' boys didn't know whether to go blind or run, so they just sat there with sheepish grins. I knew what they were thinking. Teacher is mad . . . we've ruined everything . . . he may even take the basketball goals down and rip up the ball.

"Instead, I asked who had the tobacco. One of the boys pulled a half-plug out of his pocket. I asked for it. He handed it to me and I took a chaw. I had chewed tobacco since I was thirteen years old, although I've never used tobacco on a Texas schoolground.

"Those boys were chewing tobacco before they cut their permanent teeth. They were working boys who earned their own money, I knew my clientele. That chaw of tobacco tied those boys to me as nothing else could. I got their promise that they would never take a chaw on the schoolground and never give tobacco to small boys. After I caught them and exacted that promise, it wasn't fun anymore. I doubt that they went to the woods three times during the rest of the term."

Early in that school term, my father had made clear that these boys, almost his age, were to address him as *Mr.* Carl.

"Not that it does me any good," he said, "but it will do you good to show proper respect for your superiors."

At a recent reunion of teacher and students, all old men now, my father recalled that incident. He nodded toward the creek at the edge of the community center clearing, and added, "You know, before I left here, you ol' boys would have jumped in that creek for me if I had asked you to."

"Still would, Mr. Carl," one answered, grinning.

The New Year Hasn't Always Started January 1

=============== **Archie McDonald**

The Daily Sentinel
Sunday, January 1, 1995

Happy New Year!

Many dates and symbols have marked the waning of the old and welcoming the new year, but the most difficult thing has been getting a majority of us to agree when to observe the passage.

Early peoples associated the new year with completion of a harvest and purifying of food that insured the continuation of life, so the vernal equinox, or March 25 under the ancient calendar, provided a common date for observance. Others used the summer solstice, or some date deemed appropriate to their culture.

The Romans first used January 1 to begin the new year in 153 B.C., but several centuries were required to sort out the calendar, as ordered by Julius Caesar, to make it appear more or less as it does today. In the beginning, this was simply the first day when new consuls took office in Rome.

Christian Europe clung to March 25 as their special day of renewal until Pope Gregory XIII decreed the adoption of a new calendar in 1582 that accepted January 1 as the appropriate date to commence a new year. Protestants gradually accepted the same date—Germany in 1700, Great Britain in 1752, and Sweden in

1753; even Japan and China did so in 1873 and 1912 for business purposes despite its association with Christianity.

Ancient rites associated with the New Year included purging and purification, extinguishing and rekindling fires, masked processions, fights between opposing teams, and an interlude of Carnival—excessive drinking. Many of those features survive.

At one time the event featured the giving of gifts. In Rome and in Elizabethan England, this was a kind of annual "tribute" to the emperor or king. Eventually the influence of Germany moved most of the gift giving to Christmas. It was also a time for dropping by the homes of friends, who prepared by having buffets of food and drink ready.

A special feature in America has been the Tournament of Roses in Pasadena, California, begun in 1886 by the Valley Hunt Club. The first football contest associated with the day occurred in 1902 (Michigan walloped Stanford, 49–0), but chariot races were held the next year, and the regular Rose Bowl football game did not begin until 1916.

Long before our time America set its own "standards" for New Year's, many of them more associated with New Year's Eve: Guy Lombardo and His Royal Canadians "coming to you live from the Ambassador Hotel"; the falling electric ball on Times Square; parties with dancing and champagne at midnight; blowing horns and utilizing other racket makers; license, almost a duty, to hug or kiss everyone within reach; and rigging up some older man to look like Father Time to get booted out of the way by a fresh bediapered youngster. All, in their way, celebrating survival and expectation. Then, the next day, survivors watch football, football, and football.

How will you observe the passage? I can recall a New Year's Eve camping at Blanco when we appeared to be the only living creatures on the earth, and blowing the car horn that only we could hear; dancing and staying the night at Hotel Fredonia just before it went dark for several years; a splendid evening at Cawtawa Mountain Lodge in northern Georgia when the telephone crew from Atlanta set the pace and had more fun than middle-aged folks usually are allowed.

However you observe the day and its eve, be safe, and cheer for my teams in the bowl games. You'll know which ones—they will be losing.

Valentine's Day: How It All Began

The Daily Sentinel
February 14, 1995

Will you be mine, my dearest Valentine? How this day came to be associated with the wooing of lovers is a great mystery, for most of the Saints Valentine with whom February 14 is associated as feast day—there were at least three and perhaps as many as eight—were martyrs. The best known of the lot, a priest of Rome and a Bishop of Interamna, lost their heads but not over love; their deaths came as a result of the order of Emperor Claudius II.

One story connected with these early saints strikes at least a chord of romance: one jailed St. Valentine fell in love with his keeper's daughter and sent her a letter signed "from your Valentine."

Perhaps no more accurately, early Europeans believed that birds mated on February 14 and assumed that human youth followed suit; or that the Norman word "galantin," meaning "lover of women," sounded with a "v" off the tongues of Norsemen and thus became "valentin."

Better yet, some trace the wooing and loving from the Roman feast of Lupercalia, associated with rebirth, during which names of girls were drawn by lot by young men who then regarded them as sweethearts for a year. The early Christian church objected to this practice, so for a few centuries the names of saints to be emulated were substituted. Choosing girls was more fun than saints, of course, so the practice reverted by the fourteenth century, and by then both genders did the choosing, often accompanied by the giving of gifts. Valentine's Day was by then a divination; a young girl supposedly would marry the first person she saw that day and great care had to be taken lest this view fall upon an unacceptable suitor.

Charles Duc d'Orleans gets credit for sending the first "poetical or amorous address" called a valentine, and did so from the Tower of London in 1415 as rhymed love letters to his wife.

The traditions of Valentine's Day and lovers had difficulty crossing the ocean to the American colonies, partly because "romance" often had little to do with pairing then—many women were paid to immigrate for the purpose and found matrimony waiting for the boat. And because public expression of affection was banned in Puritan areas and punished when exhibited, as when a Captain Kimble of Boston sat for two hours in the stocks for kissing his wife, no favor shown for his just returning from a three-year voyage.

I received, and sent, my first Valentine's cards in kindergarten, where we showed no favorites. Even so homely a person as I received one from everyone else. By and by we learn to discriminate, of course, and narrow the focus of our expressions of affection. Thirty-nine years or so ago, while earning college credit by participating on the debate team, I encountered a skinny, energetic, vivacious, fix-the-world, co-ed. I gave her a rose one day; she threatened me with a rock. And I haven't won a debate since.

Borrowed, with appreciation, from a nineteenth-century valentine:

A short time since I danc'd with you,
And from that hour lov'd you true;
Your pleasing form, your charming air,
Might with a fabl'd grace compare;
Your accents, so melodious sweet,
Still on my ear does seem to beat;
And 'tis the first (and last) wish of my life,
To win my Judy for a wife;
Deign, my sweet maid, a line to send,
And may love's saint my plea defend.

Columbus Day Roots Are in This Century

The Daily Sentinel
Monday, October 10, 1994

Giving Christopher Columbus his own "day" developed in the twentieth century and is a tribute as much to the millions of Italian immigrants and their descendants as to the day's namesake.

Columbus was born in 1451 in Genoa, a province in that part of Europe not destined to be known as the nation of Italy until over 400 years later. He helped his father in the weaving trade until the age of fourteen, then began what he called "navigating," meaning seafaring. In his sailings, Columbus developed the idea that it would be possible to reach the East—India, Cathay (China), or Chipango (Japan) by sailing west, a not altogether original thought, but a practical one if the Western Hemisphere had not been in the way.

Columbus petitioned his native Genoa, Portugal's King John II, even England's Henry VII, for support, before making his pitch to Ferdinand and Isabella of Spain in 1486. Even so, he did not receive a commission to begin a voyage of exploration until 1492, and a splendid commission it was. Henceforth, Columbus was

"Admiral of All the Ocean Seas," a larger command than received by any other before or since.

Columbus' flagship *Santa Maria* was joined by two caravels, *Pinta* and *Niña*, for the voyage that left Palos on August 3. After refitting in the Canary Islands, he started across the Atlantic on September 6 and had to deal not only with unknown seas but with a doubtful crew as well. Twice he changed course fortuitously; once to follow migrating birds in the belief they would find land, and once toward a mysterious "light" sighted while still so far from land that the earth's curvature would have prevented his seeing it if burning on the firmament.

On October 12, Roderigo de Triana sounded the alarm that land had been sighted. Columbus named the island San Salvador, thought by many to be what was known later as Watling Island. He named the indigenous population "Indians" because he thought, or professed to think, that he was on an island off the Indian coast.

Columbus sailed about the Caribbean, and on Cuba saw the "Indians" smoking tobacco. After grounding *Santa Maria* on a coral reef on Christmas Eve, he left for Europe on January 4, 1493, and made landfall in Portugal. Word of his return preceded him in Spain, so he was welcomed warmly, and subsequently found support for three more voyages to the New World. Apparently he never set foot on any part of North America.

And the world turned upside down. In what is called the Columbian Exchange, the wealth of the New World joined that of the Old, and in turn Europe sent its religion, languages, and other things, not all of them positive. There is yet argument about who gave who syphilis, for example. After falling from grace for a while, Columbus died with honor and wealth on May 20, 1506.

The first celebration of Columbus Day in the U. S. occurred in New York City in 1792, and then went unobserved until the 400th anniversary of Columbus' first voyage. The U. S. marked the occasion by spending ten million dollars on the World's Columbian Exposition, or World's Fair, in Chicago in 1892–93, attended by twelve million people.

Colorado was the first state to declare October 12 a state holiday, and did so in 1905; New York followed in 1909. In 1937 President Franklin D. Roosevelt proclaimed the first national Columbus Day. Since then, Italians everywhere in the U. S. have had an opportunity to show ethnic pride, much like the Irish on St. Patrick's Day.

The holiday is now observed officially on the second Monday in October.

An apocryphal story learned so long ago I could have heard Columbus himself tell it provides an excellent evaluation of Columbus' achievement: upon returning to Spain and receiving that era's equivalent of the "ticker-tape parade," disgruntled associates began to say, "All he did was run into America, it wasn't like it was a moving target," and the like. Hearing such carping at a banquet, Columbus called for a raw egg and invited all to balance it on its elliptical end. None, of course could do so, until he gently tapped it, broke the shell, and stood it on the jagged edges. All could have done so; only he knew how and when.

Texas' Oddest Animal

======================================= **Jerry Turner**

The Mexia Daily News
March 12, 1999

What has a scaled head like a lizard's, ears like a mule's, claws like a bear's, and a tail shaped like a rat's? Need more clues? What has been called a tortoise rabbit, a pig in a turtle's shell, a small tank, and a watermelon with a snake under it? Give up, or did you guess it is the Texas nine-banded armadillo?

All these descriptions fit the unusual armadillo, but it has habits just as unique as its appearance. The armored mammal can walk under water, leap into the air like a cat when startled, and is the only animal which can contract the oldest of human diseases—leprosy. About the only thing that an armadillo cannot do is what it is reported to do and that is curl itself into a ball. Maybe the only other thing an armadillo cannot do is to cross a highway.

The shy little animal is not native to Central Texas, but has extended its range during the past 100 years. Not only has it made Texas home, but it has moved as far north as Oklahoma and as far east as Mississippi. Early Texans probably never saw this strange little creature.

The armadillo has become a popular figure among modern day Texans. Some have even promoted it to be the official state

David Thomas sculpture, Lubbock Lake Landmark State Historical Park

animal, nosing out the traditional symbol—the Texas Longhorn. Armadillos are often raced at festivals. Sanctioned by The World Armadillo Breeding and Racing Association, Inc., racing 'dillos can often reach speeds of up to eight miles per hour.

For those who don't want to compete on the racetrack, armadillos, according to some fearless gourmets, are good to eat. During the Great Depression, the 'dillo was known as the "Hoover Hog" in honor of Herbert Hoover, president during those hard times. Also, called "the poor's pig," the armadillo was a source of meat when soup lines were common.

The Texas armadillo's most impressive feature is its armor. The shell is composed of ossified, scalelike skin which forms a three-piece covering for the body. The head and exposed parts are covered with the same material, while the tail is ringed by fourteen bands of armor. The underside of the critter is covered with coarse hairs. Some of the same hair can be found growing on the shell.

The adult armadillo normally has thirty-two peg-like teeth, all molars and all without enamel. Its brain is said to resemble those of the rats, opossums, and moles. The armadillo has a wide range of body temperatures. Some have been recorded with temperatures as high as ninety-five degrees and others as low as eighty-five degrees. The shell provides very little warmth or insulation.

The oddities of the armadillo do not end with its appearance or body structure. Reproduction has its own peculiarities. Armadillo mothers give birth to four babies—all of the same sex. The babies, looking like small models of their parents, feed on their mother's four nipples. They are born with their eyes open and can walk within a few hours of birth. After nursing for about two months they join their mother in probing for insects. The longest life-span for a captive armadillo is sixteen years.

Because the armadillo, unlike other mammals, cannot maintain a constant temperature, it is more active when it can be comfortable without much trouble. Temperature affects its roaming more than light. It will seek out cool places in hot summer and bed down in an underground home during cold weather.

Foraging for insects is the armadillo's chief occupation. With a highly developed sense of smell, the armadillo can find insects in the ground as deep as six inches. Once discovered, the insect, worm or grub is dug out by the powerful legs and claws. The probing follows no regular pattern and an area may be covered more than once. The excellent sense of smell is used to detect danger. While feeding, the armadillo makes a low grunting sound, much as the pig, which he resembles in his rooting.

While the armadillo was not present in Texas when early settlers arrived, out-of-state visitors are curious about this well known Texas symbol. This critter seems to hold a place of prominence when folks talk about Texas.

What Mrs. Rives Found in Gilmer

Sarah Greene

The Gilmer Mirror
January 30, 1999

During early Reconstruction the town of Gilmer, seat of Upshur County, differed culturally from its small town rural neighbors in Northeast Texas because of a unique institution situated there: the Looney School.

A South Carolina native, Morgan H. Looney, moved to Gilmer from Georgia in 1860 and established a school that he operated from 1861 to 1871 as "one of the most successful schools in Texas in that day" (D. T. Loyd in *A History of Upshur County, Texas*). It certainly had one of the most distinguished faculties. Oran M. Roberts, who had been chief justice of the secession convention that took Texas out of the Union, was elected U. S. Senator from Texas in 1866, but was denied seating because he could not take an oath that he had not supported the Confederacy. So he came to Gilmer to teach in the Looney School. Miss Achsa Culberson, a cousin of Governor Charles Culberson, taught at the school and married Morgan Looney's brother, M. L. And there were others.

Students, who came from near and far, made their marks in many ways. Among them were the Texas governor and U. S. senator, Charles A. Culberson; Sam Templeton, Texas attorney gen-

(above) A funeral procession, looking north from the Upshur County Courthouse in Gilmer in the 1890s.

(right) Morgan Looney, who operated the school that brought Mrs. Rives and many others to Gilmer in the 1860s. Photo courtesy Historic Upshur Museum

(below) The east side of the courthouse square some time in the first 15 years of this century, showing at the left corner the Masonic Hall that was here when Mrs. Reeves lived in Gilmer.

eral; Jot Gunter, prominent attorney who built San Antonio's Gunter Hotel; Governor Culberson's sister, Sallie Stinson, later the wife of Governor James Stephen Hogg.

One of the parents who moved to Gilmer to enroll her children in the Looney School, Mary Elizabeth Carter Rives, made the trip by buggy from her home in Louisiana. She left a diary of her Gilmer years that is a part of the Southern Historical Collection in the Wilson Library, the University of North Carolina at Chapel Hill.

Arriving in Gilmer with her sister, Anna, in September, 1868, Mrs. Rives was warmly welcomed by the local gentry, her diary reflects. The two soon settled into a routine of making and receiving calls, attending any church that was having a service on a given Sunday (no visiting on Sabbath), quilting, visiting the sick, sewing, gardening and working with the hired cook on food preservation and preparing meals. Judge Roberts had purchased the house opposite her, "so I will have good neighbors," she wrote.

The diary reflects that both Mrs. Rives's mood and her physical well being depended on the vagaries of East Texas weather.

On October 19 she wrote: "More rain, no sunshine, no company, no news, no boxes from Shreveport. Well, we can get along a little while longer, if the weather is not too cold." By November 10 it was "cold, cold tonight. Effie [her niece] almost had a chill."

November 14 brought the welcome news that supply wagons had arrived at Mr. Boyd's store. The Rives household acquired "a large box full of nice good things to eat and wear, two hams, two gallons whisky, vinegar, rice, sugar (crushed), cheese, black pepper, soda, sage, coffee, milk, washboards and some fruit and candy, clothes for the boys, etc., besides several good letters and a bonnet for me."

Gilmer had never been as affluent as neighboring Pittsburg, Jefferson or Marshall, so post-war hard times were different only in degree. But rainy days and cold weather were downers for the

Louisiana visitor. On rainy October 16, 1868, she wrote that the weather note was "all I have to record, no excitement of any kind, no company and worst of all I cannot get any butter and eggs. This is a poor town and country, perhaps I am the poor folks, though I beg to pay the price for these necessities."

Mrs. Rives's initial good impression of Professor Looney was confirmed on September 19 when she attended the first of many lectures at his school, which she referred to as "the college." She heard him speak to the composition class on "Habit is the stuff of which life is wove."

"It was a pretty good speech. I shall try to go every Saturday," she resolved.

In November she attended Mr. Looney's talk on "The Universal Agent," and judged it "very fine." On a cold day in early December her diary reflected "nothing to write" and she asked, "what is there in Gilmer to see, or learn." But the next day she wrote of an evening at the college where "I was never so well entertained. Three young men spoke . . . Mr. Looney was called for and I never heard such a speech . . . the music was splendid."

Concerts were frequently attended by 2,000, students read their compositions and there were visiting lecturers. One such was a Mr. Willifred, lecturer on phrenology, who "examined several heads and gave a tolerably correct guess at the character of the gentlemen."

In the nineteenth century Texas countryside we know that dancing was proscribed and "play parties" were the euphemistic substitute. Not so in sophisticated Gilmer. On December 19, the last day of the fall semester, Mrs. Rives heard five speeches and splendid music, and then, "The girls, Mr. Aldridge and Claude [her son] went and danced. . . . Of course it was a gay time. "

This was anything but usual. According to Loyd's *History of Upshur County*, classrooms were segregated by gender and the young men could make calls on the young women only when the rules were suspended. The rules included no swearing, gambling, dancing, drinking or horse racing.

In the midst of holiday preparations Mrs. Rives noted that she and her niece Effie had finished reading Milton's *Paradise Lost*, and "the more we read the better pleased we are with that grandest of poets." They had begun Byron's *Cain* and planned to read as much as possible during Christmas vacation. But on Christmas Eve company came for dinner and stayed to dance until midnight.

Her Christmas day entry reported an all-day headache, "effects of sitting up so late and frolicking." But it didn't keep her from serving eggnog to guests.

The next year began with parties and a ball, for which Mrs. Rives helped Mrs. Boyd bake a cake. Three days later the party season ended as classes resumed at the Looney School and "the rules" were back in place. Mrs. Rives went to hear "Mr. Looney lecture and read the rules, all very good, first rate, excellent. He shall have all my little influence, my heart cooperating and concurrence in his undertaking. I sincerely hope the school will be full and flourishing." But the weather was freezing cold and she was out of wood.

The 1868–69 school year ended with frigid winter giving way to an abnormally cold spring. Chills, fevers, bad colds, headaches and rheumatism plagued Mrs. Rives and members of her household, often keeping them inside on the days when they would have liked to attend Mr. Looney's lectures and other programs at the college. Fortunately there was no repetition of the "congestive chill" that carried away Mrs. Pahn's three-year-old daughter Lillie the month the Rives party arrived, but there were adult deaths from unspecified reasons.

On June 10, 1869, "one of the saddest days I have ever spent," Mrs. Rives's dear friend Mrs. Ogilvie died "after the most intense suffering," despite which she demonstrated "such resignation, such calmness and such a triumphant departure" with many friends standing around her bed. ("Last words" were highly valued in the custom of that time.)

Mrs. Rives left Gilmer in 1870 to make her home in Shreveport. She lived until 1900, but her diary had only occasional entries after the Gilmer interlude.

Dated 1869 were several "cures" she acquired in Gilmer, including this one:

A CERTAIN CURE FOR SMALLPOX AND SCARLET FEVER

Sulphate of zinc, one grain; foxglove (digitalis), one grain; half a teaspoonful of sugar; mix with two tablespoons of water. When they are thoroughly mixed add four ounces of water.

Take a spoonful every hour, either disease will disappear in twelve hours. For a child smaller doses, according to age.

If you value advice and experience, use this, for the terrible disease.

He "Woodn't" Trade Hobby for Anything

================================ **John Fooks**

The Texarkana Gazette
August 29, 1998

About five years ago, Buddy Jones was out hunting with his son in Longview, Texas, when he got an idea for the perfect Christmas present for his wife, Shirley Fay.

He had been sitting under a pine tree, relaxing and waiting for a deer to come tromping by, when the sight of the pine cones sparked a memory he retained from serving overseas in the South Pacific during World War II.

He had noticed the Japanese often decorated the roofs of their houses with tile or straw. Looking at the pine cones, he wondered if there might be something similar he could do with them.

By the time he got home, he had it all worked out in his mind: a cedar keepsake chest, shaped in the form of a house, with a peaked roof covered with broken-off scales of pine cones.

Somewhere along the way he had another idea for the cedar chest house: Cover the outside walls with crushed petrified wood that he had collected off his brother-in-law's forty acres of land near Leola, Arkansas.

He knew he had a pretty good idea, but he had no idea how good.

When his wife, two daughters and son saw what he had done, they were amazed.

Daughter Sherry Brackeen saw a future.

"He's always been good with his hands, and I've been selling his stuff out of my place (Tangles Hair Salon) for about five years now," Brackeen said.

"But his cedar chest houses are incredible; you have to see one to believe how unique and beautiful they are. We're going to enter one into the Four States Fair this year."

Although it takes five full workdays to build one—and he glues some 1,600 individual pine cone scales on each roof by hand—he's built fifty or sixty chests since he first got the idea and there's still a demand for them.

Like most men who develop the hobby of woodworking after retirement, Jones showed a penchant for it when he was a boy.

He made many of his own toys and built a wooden go-cart that he pedaled everywhere. He'd see something he liked and would eyeball it for measurements, or use his hands and arms for measurements.

Then he'd draw a few working plans and use them throughout the building process.

His technique hasn't changed much ever since.

"I'll cut out a picture in a magazine of something I like or something I think would sell in my shop and take it to my dad," Brackeen said.

"He'll look at the picture, estimate the dimensions and measurements, draw up some plans and build it from scratch. You can't tell the difference between the one he builds and the one in the photograph."

Brackeen, herself a country arts and crafts painter and decorator, usually takes his finished pieces and does the finishing or painting herself.

Her salon is replete with Grandma jelly cupboards, hand crafted

Mission furniture, old-time wash stands, rockers, Victorian beds, six-legged dining tables like those from the 1880s, bird houses, bookcases, flour bin cupboards, squirrel feeders, butterfly houses, picture frames, fake water wells (for the front yard), pictures and paintings.

One customer said stepping into Brackeen's shop is "like stepping into Grandma's attic." She calls her woodworking business Attic Illusions.

Jones, seventy-four, retired from the U. S. Army after twenty years of service then retired from Red River Army depot after twenty years as a mechanic. Through the years he has tried a number of things, from oil painting (for which he's won ribbons and recognitions) to writing short stories.

He and his wife have been married fifty-one years, and they remodeled the house they live in today out in Liberty Eylau Community near Lake Wright Patman.

After retirement from Red River, they built his woodworking shop. The shop is complete with everything he needs to build just about anything he—or his daughter—might want.

"During the summer I'm usually out working in the shop from early morning until about 11:30 A.M.," Jones said. "During the winter, I'll work all day long and come in after dark—or until my wife says I've done enough for that day."

The Ghosts of Bill Longley

==

A. C. Greene

The Dallas Morning News
January 3, 1999

The Fall 1998 issue of *UTA Magazine* of the University of Texas at Arlington, told how geology professor Brooks Ellwood and his crew made an interesting and convincing case that, after an earlier fruitless search by the Smithsonian Institution, they had finally located the grave of Texas outlaw William Preston (Bill) Longley.

The grave contained sufficient evidence to establish that Bill Longley had (1) died from his legal hanging in 1878 and (2) was buried at Giddings, Texas, the site of his hanging. Although legend persisted that he escaped the noose and a hog was substituted in his casket, the UT-Arlington findings seem to take care of that theory.

However, I am sure the discovery of the grave, while it may disprove suppositions that Bill had escaped to South America or that he lived out a long and law-abiding life in Louisiana under the name Brown, will not end theories that the bones found buried were not Bill Longley's—or other mistaken identity rumors.

I have a sixty-six-year-old clipping from the long defunct *Houston Press* which reports an interview with Hiram G. Craig of

Brenham and Coleman, and Bill McClellan, of Houston, both present at the Longley hanging.

"There used to be a saying that the only critter with more lives than a cat was a Southwest bad man—Jesse James, Billie [sic] the Kid and Bill Longley have been coming to life from all parts of the compass."

Mr. Craig began, "It was on October 11, 1878, and it was as sad a scene as ever I saw in my life. I was twenty-three years old at the time and it was the first hanging I'd seen. It was a very hot day. The gallows was set up about 600 yards north of town and there was ropes stretched around it to hold the people back. I took my station early where I could see everything and hear every word said. At the time set, we saw the hack [carrying Longley] drawn by two horses come across the railroad tracks. Bill McClellan was in that hack."

Bill McClellan reported, "I had signed up as a deputy under Sheriff Jim Brown after horse thieves and cow thieves had stole me out. I was one of the men that took Bill Longley to [prison in] Galveston and I went with Sheriff Brown to bring him back. He was as biddable a prisoner as ever I handled. I got to be right chummy with him on those trips. We went to the same school but Bill was somewhat older than I was."

Mr. Craig put in, "He came of good people. Old Man Longley was a good Christian."

Mr. McClellan agreed. "We used to go fifteen miles to camp meeting and Old Man Longley was always there. He wrote several hymns they used to sing."

(above left) William Preston Longley, photo taken in Galveston, October 1877. Courtesy Western History Collection, University of Oklahoma Library

(above right) In June 1877, a manacled Bill Longley is flanked by Deputy Bill Burrows (l.) and Sheriff Milton Mast (r.). Courtesy East Texas Research Center, Stephen F. Austin State University, Nacogdoches, Texas

(right) Bill Longley addresses the crowd from the gallows (from *National Police Gazette*, 26 October 1878, and courtesy Chuck Parsons, Smiley, Texas)

Bill Longley on the Gallows

The Dallas Morning News
January 10, 1999

William Preston Longley was hanged in 1878, but until his "lost" grave was found, myths concerning the outlaw's death abounded. Bill McClellan, a sheriff's deputy, accompanied Bill Longley to the gallows.

Hiram G. Craig described an incident at the gallows: "Bill, when you and Z. P. Eggleston [another deputy] walked onto the gallows steps, right behind Longley, it made too much weight on it. The steps began to shake when he was about half way up and he said, 'Look out, there—let's don't get crippled up before the show is over!'"

Longley's last act was to smoke a cigar. Another account reported Bill Longley spoke low but had a fine voice that carried to everybody listening.

"Well," he said, "I haven't much to say. I have to die. I hate to die. We all hate it when the time comes, but I guess those I killed hated to die as bad as I do and I have made my peace with my God. I see a good many enemies around me and mighty few friends. If I have any friends here I hope they will do nothing to avenge my death. If they want to avenge my death, let them pray for me. I deserve this fate. It is a debt I owe for my wild reckless life. I forgive everybody and I hope you all will forgive me. I have nothing more to say."

A prayer was said, and then Bill Longley did a very unlooked for thing. He kissed Sheriff Jim Brown and then the preacher.

He raised a hand and in a clear ringing voice called, "Goodbye, everybody!" He nodded to the hangman, who looked like he was pretty nervous, standing there waiting with the rope.

The black cap was pulled over Bill Longley's head, the rope was thrown up over the 4 x 4 beam and the signal was given. The rope was tied in a slip knot because nobody in Giddings knew how to tie a hangman's noose.

When Bill Longley dropped through the trap door, the rope slipped and his feet struck the ground under the platform so hard his knees buckled. Three official doctors took eleven minutes to declare him dead. One turned Bill Longley's neck around almost 360 degrees.

Dr. Longsdon mounted the gallows steps and threw up his hands as if to say, "It's all over!"

A witness said, "At first there was just a kind of silence as if we were waiting for more news. Then somebody in the crowd gave a cough that sounded to the rest of us like a laugh, and the entire bunch began laughing until for a minute it sounded like we was trying to whoop poor Bill Longley's soul right off to hell. There was more than one of us had us a case of chill-bumps right there."

Haunted by Bill Longley

The Dallas Morning News
January 17, 1999

In my growing up years I was more than partially raised by Mrs. Mary Catherine Longley, my great-grandmother. Thus, for much of my early life I thought I was a Longley. By the time I realized my kinship to the Longley family was one of marriage, not of blood, it was too late.

I had heard, and absorbed, too much of Bill Longley, the out-law, who bragged that he killed thirty-two men—and some said a woman. I did think I might be kin of Campbell Longley, his father (and a San Jacinto veteran).

The Longley "connection" began many years before I was born when, in 1890, my great-grandmother, a twenty-eight-year-old widow with four children, married seventy-year-old Campbell Longley, a music teacher in Nolanville, Bell County, who taught his musicians by means of a parlor organ.

My grandmother Maude, then eleven years old, took violin lessons from him. The marriage was not a love match, but had been instigated by the participants' families: the Longleys figured their old father needed someone to look after him, his first wife, Bill's mother, having passed away several years before.

The young widow, Mary Catherine Dockray Craighead, had no particular job skills—she wasn't a schoolteacher or dressmaker or trained for any of the limited female occupations available in Bell County.

So her family, faced with supporting her and her four children, also breathed a sigh of relief. (I later learned, *not* from my great-grandmother, you may be sure, that she had demanded that there be no hanky-panky, but on their wedding night, elderly feet in carpet slippers came shuffling down the hall. . . .)

The May and December marriage was not a success. After three years they separated; but both were members of the Church of Christ, which sanctioned divorce in few instances, so they never divorced and Mary Catherine was Mrs. Longley the rest of her eighty-two years.

Cam Longley, as he was called, had a married daughter also named Mary Catherine Longley (Tyler), who was older than the widow. This similarity in names has led to misassumptions by historians.

She supposedly was the one who wrote letters (which my great-grandmother saw years later), allegedly from Bill, telling the old mother that he was alive in South America. However, Campbell Longley never denied his son's death by the rope.

I heard all sorts of Longley stories as a boy, but I thought there was no way that the outlaw ever had an occasion to encounter my great-grandmother. But on moving to Salado, in Bell County, I discovered that on two occasions the Longley family had lived in Salado or around; once before, then after, Bill's hanging.

And I further discovered, so had my great-grandmother. All being members of the same small church, I am sure Mary Catherine, though a teenager on the first occasion (she first married at age sixteen), knew the Longleys.

One of Bill Longley's little personal tales (his autobiography is filled with a sort of cool arrogance) concerns a visit to Salado, a price on his head, to visit his parents. As he was riding out of the village, four young men attempted to capture him for the reward. He turned on them and his deadly reputation and his scathing tongue scared them away. He bragged he didn't even unholster his pistol.

Vada Sutton, Clerk of Bell County, made me copies of the 1890 marriage licenses not only for Old Cam and Mary Catherine but for my grandmother Maude Craighead and Ambrose H. Cole in 1897.

Young Maude got along well with the Longleys when her mother was living with Cam, although there were a couple of tense nights when two Longley boys thought the house on the Lampasas River was about to be raided by Mary Catherine's Dockray brothers to whom she had appealed for help, claiming she was being held prisoner.

My grandmother told how the shades were drawn and by candlelight the Longleys molded bullets to repel the Dockrays. The latter boys were as tough as the Longleys. That crisis passed without bloodshed, and Old Cam wrote a nice little inscription in Maude's schoolgirl autograph book—but she said she hated to kiss him because his beard was stained with snuff.

Weather Lore Isn't All Wet

Stanley Marcus

The Dallas Morning News
June 17, 1997

If fat squirrels, red skies and mackerel clouds sound like a bad dream, then you obviously need to brush up on your down-home weather lore.

Low-flying bats, rainbows in the west, aching teeth, mackerel skies, fat squirrels, sun dogs, red skies at night, and croaking frogs all have something in common. They are staples of weather lore. Some of it is as old as the Bible, but it is also as modern as today's amateur meteorologists.

With today's modern, computerized weather equipment, we may likely scoff at ancient weather sayings. Our skyscraper offices and temperature-controlled houses keep us nicely insulated, but the early farmers and ancient mariners who depended on them for their safety and livelihoods may have the last laugh yet, because a lot of these cornball forecasts are actually based on scientific facts.

For example, a ring around the moon does mean that rain will come, usually within twenty-four hours. A line around a car wash often produces the same result. On a spring or fall evening, vapor rising from a river means that frost is coming. This does not apply,

however, to mist rising from heated swimming pools. A morning rainbow in the west has nothing scientific to do with midgets or witches, but it does mean that rain is coming soon.

You can count on a January thaw— especially if an ice storm snaps the power lines to your deep freezer. And, last, frogs do croak more just before rain, but I can tell you from personal experience that crickets chirp more after they're inside the house!

Our nightly exposure to the professional weather forecasts on TV is having the effect of dulling our observation of nature's signals. We prefer to watch the weather recap being explained with apparent authority by a commentator who appears to be an expert. Since no credentials are offered prior to the forecasts, I believe it's wise to be a bit skeptical until the announcer proves to be right at least three out of four broadcasts.

Weather lore is more than a lot of hot air, even if most of the predictions are accurate only to within twenty-four hours. But so what? Accurate predictions are often beyond the scope of professional meteorologists, too.

The public's obsession with weather reports has always puzzled me. Aside from knowing whether rain or snow is predicted, I find very little actual value that the information provides.

Animals Dominate Our Language

Stanley Marcus

The Dallas Morning News
February 12, 1985

Medieval calligraphers on up to contemporary book printers have enjoyed the typographical exercise of creating books with animal illustrations. Occasionally, the animals, twenty-six in number, were related to the letters of the alphabet, viz, C as in cat, D as in dog, etc. Such books carry the name "bestiaries."

Although I've been using the English language, for better for worse, during eighty of my eighty-two years, I had not realized how much our vocabulary has drawn upon the names of animals, fowl and insects to enrich the imagery of our conversations.

We use these words daily and so frequently that we become totally unaware of our practice. If, for example, we want to express complete exhaustion, we say "dog tired," or if we choose to describe a well-used book, we refer to it as "dogeared." Golf players usually bemoan a "dogleg" hole. Hot weather means "the dog days," and a man of my age might be referred to as "a gay old dog," long past the state of "puppy love."

If we have a "black sheep" in the family, we refer to him as "gone to the dogs," but if he doesn't cause us too much trouble, we might tend to ignore him with the explanation of "let sleeping dogs lie." We have "hawks" and "doves," both of which can be "mulish" in their attitudes. As long as they don't make "asses" of themselves, we can tolerate them. If we want to buy an impressive gift for a loved one, we might buy a "cat's-eye" ring or we might just send some "tiger lilies."

We use animals' and fowls' names, not only as adjectives like "catty," "kittenish," "bullish," and "bearish," but also as plain verbs such as "rat on a friend," "hog the spotlight," "cow a witness," and "goose a companion."

We use them as standards of comparison, such as "slippery as an eel," "proud as a peacock," "sly as a fox," "wise as an owl," "meek as a lamb," "stubborn as a mule," "strong as an ox," and "crooked as a snake." If we play our gin game "doggedly," we can avoid being "skunked." But experienced gamblers avoid "card sharks," unless they're carrying a "rabbits foot."

We describe a teen-ager as having a "ducktail," a chief executive as being "top dog," intemperate men as "wild bulls," a Lothario as a "tomcat," a pallid lass as "mousy," a second-term president as a "lame duck," a lone sentry as a "sitting duck," an unattractive child as an "ugly duckling," and a marital ex as a "louse."

Our hitless ball team scores a "goose egg" because one of the players "loused up a throw to first." In such a case, runs are "scarce as hens' teeth." If we "smell a rat," we're apt to "let the cat out of the bag." If we are terrifically hungry, we can become "pigs" as we "wolf" down a meal.

The news editor waits for the "bulldog edition" before he "bulldozes" the front page. We beware of "quacks," but when we like something, we might call it the "cat's meow." That is better than being referred to as a "cat's-paw."

If we don't "chicken" out in life, there's always the chance we might end up being "top dog." Much as man esteems his best friend, the dog, he labels a bad-selling article derogatively as a "dog," and if he's a theatrical producer, he prefers to eat a chicken sandwich, for a "turkey" is a synonym for a complete flop. People who "ape" or "parrot" others gain the reputation of being "copy-cats." A good way to avoid that epithet is to sit "catty-cornered" with your back to the simian and polly.

When we go to the flicks to see a "horse opera," we don't "put on the dog." Instead, we don a pair of slacks and a "houndstooth" patterned jacket. If a judge hears completely fresh evidence, he might well comment, "That's a horse of a different color."

We place a bet or buy a stock when we get a tip "right out of the horse's mouth." We used to "walk a mile for a Camel," unless we were suffering from a "charley horse." When we need a mild expletive, we say, "Doggone it."

If I had any "horse sense," I'd go "bell the cat"; I should "duck out" and quit "horsing around."

"Horsefeathers" or "rats"—as the case may be—if I don't feel better in the morning, I'll take a shot of the "hair of the dog that bit me."

Brilliant Brickmanship

Allan Turner

Houston Chronicle
Sunday, May 26, 1996

REDFORD—The old man, his knees stiff with arthritis, hobbled from the blazing afternoon into the cool, dusky interior of his boyhood home. Bordering on ramshackle, it was just another of the dun-colored, mud-brick structures that dot this desert land along the Rio Grande. It was a home for goats.

Shifting the white cowboy hat on his bald, sweat-beaded head, the man scanned the kitchen's smoke-marred walls, the straw on the floor.

"You see," he began in heavily accented English, "the inside still is good. Most of this house was here when my father came in 1911. How long will adobe last? Oh, mamacita! It will last 200 years—if it's good adobe, you mix it right and you keep it dry."

The man knows adobe well. He was born in this house, third room on the end, seventy-five years ago this July. He is Carmen Orozco, this region's most famous adobero—adobe folk architect and builder.

From the Institute of Texan Cultures in San Antonio to the Smithsonian Institution in Washington, D. C., Orozco is hailed as a brilliant master of his craft. His was the guiding vision in restoring the massive 1848 Fort Leaton in Presidio, a project that took four years to complete and involved the manufacture and placement of 80,000 adobe bricks.

But in Redford and neighboring Presidio, where he has spent his entire life, Orozco is known to his neighbors as a simple rancher, town character and home-grown philosopher. They see him every weekday morning drinking coffee at Las Palmas Restaurant after taking his fifteen-year-old daughter to school.

They know him for his good-natured jokes, his work in the Baptist Church and his nocturnal tramps through the countryside in search of buried Spanish treasure.

If they know he's famous, they don't let on.

Even Orozco seemed nonplussed by his fame. Asked if others on the Texas side of the Rio Grande handled adobe with his skill, he demurs. Maybe he is the best in Redford, his hometown, but he is a relative newcomer in Presidio.

"There may be people living back here around Presidio who do the work," he said. "I don't know them all. I have only lived in Presidio twenty-five years."

Adobe is the ideal building material for southern Presidio County, where annual rainfall barely tops ten inches—Houston's yearly average is forty-six—and summer temperatures reach 117 degrees.

"By contemporary terms," said Pat Jasper, director of Austin-based Texas Folklife Resources, which employed Orozco in its folkarts apprenticeship program, "adobe is one of the most earth-friendly architectural forms. It's completely replenishable; it's totally climatologically appropriate."

The bricks, normally twelve-by-eighteen-by-three inches, are a magnificent shield against the summer sun and a warm earthen blanket in the depths of winter. The record low for a Presidio winter is four degrees.

"It's hard work to begin with, but they're the best houses," Orozco said. "It's more cool. Adobe is our mother. It is dirt. She protects against the sun. She defends her sons, yes."

College professors believe the architectural form came to the Southwest with the Spanish conquerors centuries ago. Similar structures were common in rural Spain. To Orozco, such academic speculation seems irrelevant. He learned the craft from his father, who learned it from his father, who had come from Mexico in the 1880s to farm and work as a freighter in the Shafter silver mines. In his midteens, Orozco apprenticed himself to a friend of the family to learn the trade.

For those men, Orozco said, building with adobe simply was a life skill. Orozco was born in a house repaired and modified by his father; he now lives in an adobe house he constructed with the help of his family. Among his greatest accomplishments—one he still proudly shows visitors—is a tiny house he built for his aged mother.

Much of the adobe work Orozco performs is repair. With notable exceptions, adobe construction slowly is giving way to building with cinder block and other inexpensive modern materials. Orozco is contemptuous of the trend.

"Cinder block," he said, "is hot in summer and cold in winter."

And he is dismayed by the reluctance of young men to take up the work. "Young people," he sniffed, "they get food stamps and they don't want to learn nothing. My family, they are hard workers. What I do, they do. Lay adobe."

Thus, Orozco has continued his long-standing family tradition, teaching his thirty-year-old daughter, Rosa Holguin, the fine points of the craft.

"He had me working since I was seven," said Holguin, who now lives in Odessa. "Pulling nails out of wood and, like, mixing the dirt and keeping it moist. Things like that. We'd do everything. We'd work fixing adobes; we'd gather them, put them up and later on we'd take them and make a house. It is a hard work, but when you love it, you don't mind."

In addition to her early training in adobe work, Holguin was paired with her father in the Texas Folklife Resources' apprenticeship program.

"He is a magnificent craftsman," Jasper said. "There's really a science to building with adobe, and he was able to pass along some of the finer points, specific wisdom and traditional techniques. He was concerned with making sure that the knowledge is passed on in his family."

Orozco's home is a testament to his children's construction skills, and he enjoys explaining the nuances of rock-laying technique. Good adobe work is sturdy and subtle, its intricacies hidden beneath a thick layer of lime plaster. Bad work becomes apparent in a few years—eroding walls, falling plaster.

For sound adobe construction, three elements are crucial: good dirt, good foundation and patience.

Good dirt, Orozco said, is salt-free, contains little sand and has a clay content of at least twenty percent. A practiced hand can judge good dirt by mixing it with water and "cutting" it with a hoe.

The adobe mud is mixed, allowed to stand and mixed again. Later, wheat or oat straw is added and the raw adobe mixed yet again.

After the "batter" has reached the proper consistency, it is placed in wooden molds and allowed to harden in the desert sun for about three days.

Moisture is the natural enemy of mud brick, and a good rock foundation is crucial to a building's survival. "It's very important that no moisture goes up from the foundation to the adobe," he said. Sloppy foundation work will cause a structure to disintegrate within a few years.

Patience is a factor in every step.

Many proud new homeowners, Orozco noted, want to finish the job right away. Once the bricks are in place, they want to plaster the building inside and out. But when they do, the adobero warned, "the plaster will crack and slide down."

"You have to wait a year before you put the plaster on," he said. "You have to let the building dry and settle good—if you don't, you'll have big problems."

Orozco was concerned that rushing construction would adversely affect his greatest work, the restoration of Benjamin Leaton's massive fortified residence and trading post built in 1848 on the outskirts of present-day Presidio. The master later relented, acknowledging that while aspects of construction could have been better, the overall building is remarkably sound.

The forty-room residence now is the centerpiece of the Fort Leaton State Historical Park. Superintendent Luis Armendariz recalled that the building, which had been the home of transients since being abandoned in 1926, was in serious disrepair when Orozco was hired to oversee the effort.

"A lot of the adobes had eroded," Armendariz said, "and some of the walls had to be totally replaced." Eighty thousand bricks, he said, were prepared on-site from dirt brought in from an adobe quarry. Orozco's crew of more than twenty men worked four years to finish the work. The park opened in 1978.

"He is a character," Armendariz said of Orozco. "He was always rushing and rushing. Now he moves in little steps. He has arthritis. Now he uses his tone of voice" to convey his energy.

Even though arthritis has slowed him down, Orozco still works at his Redford ranch. He still is known for his leisurely rambles through Presidio's tiny business district, where his morning itinerary involves numerous stops for chats with friends.

Orozco still has dreams, and he shares them with all who will listen. He hopes to install a great adobe-making plant at his Redford ranch, using a commercial concrete truck as his mixer. With that arrangement, he said, he could make 1,000 bricks a day.

Or, perhaps, if he gets lucky, he will finally capture the Spanish treasures that have eluded him and his friends for decades.

Or maybe he'll realize another dream: digging a pond and turning his desert ranch into a fishing mecca.

"People always like to fish," he mused. "This would be a great place for them to come."

History as Close as a Turntable

Allan Turner

Houston Chronicle
Sunday, November 16, 1986

The gusts of winter played havoc with the old man's over-coats—three of them, spotted, threadbare and bulging—as he gripped his battered guitar and sailed down Crawford Street from the Union Station.

To passers-by who scattered at his approach that winter afternoon nearly four decades ago, the man was just another in the shabby army of beggar-musicians peopling the streets of Southern cities.

But to Mack McCormick—a nineteen-year-old jazz aficionado whose later research into black music would make him one of the nation's foremost cultural historians—the man was nothing less than walking history, a romantic, rail-rambling bard.

"As a kid, I had seen black men on street corners in Deep Ellum (Dallas' Elm Street). They were itinerant, sometimes hobos, sometimes well-dressed. There'd be these men with funny hats—that was very common; guys played guitar with gloves on.

"When I spotted him, I thought, 'Why don't I go up and talk to him?' For me, it was pure romance. He represented the freedom of walking into a freight yard and leaving town."

The musician, gruff, proud "sufficiently old and strange," viewed McCormick as a possible source of revenue. He was brusque but spoke of his recent arrival by rail and of a long-ago recording career. McCormick's questions sent him on frantic, fumbling searches through his pockets. "He had an apartment in there," McCormick recalled.

At one point, the musician inventoried the contents of his pockets, placing each item—eyeglasses, string, wire, patches of colored cloth, a can opener—on the windowsill of a Catholic school against which he leaned. At another point, dissatisfied with the tone of a peculiar metal whistle he played in accompaniment to his guitar, he dug through his pockets until he produced a hammer, which he used to tap the whistle back into tune.

The man's appearance, his performance and, to a lesser extent, his music—which was hopelessly out of tune—delighted the sizable audience that had gathered. The musician was pleased with the crowd. A crowd meant money. McCormick was a bit apprehensive. "I kept wondering when the nuns were going to show up," he said.

Today, McCormick believes the man—then in his mid-seventies—was Henry Thomas, a Northeast-Texas-born musician who recorded as Henry Thomas "Ragtime Texas" for the Vocalion label in the late 1920s.

For a black-music enthusiast, a chance encounter with Thomas—one of the most significant figures of prewar blues—would be tantamount to a student of impressionism bumping into Claude Monet at McDonald's. McCormick found the meeting disappointing, yet unforgettable.

A conversation with McCormick, a genial, slightly paunchy man of middle age, is far-ranging, jumping from his meeting with Thomas to his peripatetic boyhood, to his growing fascination with folk culture, to the work of the 1930s Farm Security Administration photographers, to the woodcarvers of Cordova, New Mexico,

Mack McCormick with a set of pan-pipes like the ones Henry Thomas recorded on.

to his decade spent with the Smithsonian, to the idiosyncrasies of obscure folk musicians, to the baseball players of San Pedro de Macores, Dominican Republic, to the sad focus in a recent television documentary on the drug problems (rather than the artistic beauty) of jazz vocalist Billie Holiday.

McCormick was the man who, in 1960, "discovered" and recorded the beloved Navasota musician Mance Lipscomb. It was he who brought Houston bluesman Samuel "Lightnin'" Hopkins to a wider audience. And it was because of McCormick that the joyful music of the late Austin pianist Robert Shaw was preserved on record and that the so-called "Santa Fe" group of barrelhouse pianists, a product of Houston's Fourth Ward, was explored and documented.

McCormick was the man who interviewed the murderer of Robert Johnson, the titanic Mississippi musician whose discs on the Vocalion label remain classics fifty years after their recording. And it likely will be McCormick who—after the killer dies—ends the mystery surrounding the womanizing guitarist who sold his soul to the devil for a song.

McCormick, who lives with his wife, Mary, and their fifteen-year-old daughter, Susannah, in a pleasant, ranch-style home in Spring Branch, describes himself as someone from "every part of the United States, especially Texas."

In fact, he was born in Pittsburgh in 1930, the only child of Gregg and Effie McCormick, a husband-wife team of X-ray technicians. His parents divorced in 1933, and the remainder of his childhood and adolescence was spent between them.

His father returned to Texas, but his mother—a woman in what was then a man's trade—traveled from town to town seeking any work she could find. She often worked as a waitress, secretary or receptionist in such communities as Cleveland, St. Louis, Dallas, Houston and Searcy, Arkansas.

"I was struck by the contrast," McCormick said. "Each was trained to do the same thing, but she was saving nickels and dimes. He bought new Buicks."

In 1939, McCormick lived with his mother and stepfather in Pritchard, Alabama, where the family operated a chicken farm. Ultimately, McCormick's mother found employment as an X-ray technician with osteopaths, and she moved to Houston.

"Growing up, I never spent two consecutive years in the same school," McCormick said.

It was while moving from place to place that he became aware—painfully aware—of regional cultural differences. In the South, he was viewed as a smart-aleck Yankee; in the North, a tough Southerner spoiling for a fight. He was the perpetual outsider, and fights were common.

His work life—including stints as a cab driver, a Las Vegas casino shill and an emergency room orderly—began early.

In 1946, McCormick worked as a ticket taker at an Ohio Lake Erie resort that featured white dance bands, including Woody Herman and Bobby Sherwood. On other occasions, he made his way to a black club in Toledo to hear musicians Nat Cole, Earl Bostic and Charlie Parker.

Two years later, he found himself in New Orleans, where he was befriended by jazz record collectors, encountered first-generation jazzmen—those who through luck or misfortune had stayed behind—and assisted Orin Blackstone in compiling his seminal discography of jazz records.

Back in Texas in 1949, McCormick—then Houston correspondent for *down beat* magazine—played a prominent role in founding the Houston Jazz Appreciation Society.

The society's 150 members—black and white—met regularly at the Club Matinee, a black nightclub owned by Houston music promoter Don Robey.

"We had afternoon meetings for more than a year, and nothing happened—blacks and whites meeting together," McCormick said. Robey, the pistol-packing owner of Peacock Records—a successful regional race label—must have been amused at the brash, young integrationist, McCormick surmised.

"No one was integrating in those days, but we never had a problem, largely because blacks were willing to let us visit their clubs and churches," he said.

Reared in the South, McCormick was aware of the roots of segregation, the nation's legacy of racism. Yet, he seemed surprised when he saw it in practice or saw the apprehension of it reflected in others' practices.

Tommy Dorsey came in for criticism in a *down beat* magazine article authored by McCormick when Dorsey replaced his black trumpeter, Charlie Shavers, with a pickup musician during a Houston appearance.

"He denied us the opportunity of hearing Charlie Shavers. He just assumed this was the South and that an integrated band wouldn't be tolerated, although others had traveled through with mixed bands without incident," McCormick said.

A few years later, McCormick fostered integration through promotion of a jazz concert and dance for a mixed audience.

The concert in the old City Auditorium featured Count Basie and Ella Fitzgerald, and throughout the evening, McCormick discreetly advised police to seat blacks and whites separately. But, he recalled, he gave each officer conflicting instructions, with the result being an integrated house.

"The police were scratching their heads," he said. "There were laws on the books against that type of thing. But it's funny. If you don't call too much attention to something, you may not have a problem."

His wife, Mary, describes McCormick as "a writer who's gone astray," and he cheerfully admits that the need to gather information while it's still available has cut into his writing time. "The question becomes whether to take time to write or to go out and interview one more person."

"I found (guitarist) Little Hat Jones literally on his deathbed," McCormick said. "He was so eager to tell what he knew. I asked him how he got the nickname 'Little Hat.' He said, 'Why, I wore it tipping it up on my head like Charlie Chaplin'—little stories like that."

While it might be tempting to concentrate on the quirky, colorful personalities of the stars, those black musicians who achieved some financial success through recording, McCormick believes the full value of an artist can be appreciated only by understanding the culture from which he sprang.

"It's not (white guitarist) Doc Watson who's important, but rather what he represents," McCormick said. "I'm more interested in seeing things in context, county by county—the total idea of musical tradition."

In 1958, he began a county-by-county survey of Texas that was to last more than eight years. "Since recordings or other documentation had been on a hit-or-miss basis, we had a tattered, incomplete picture," he said. "I was interested in a complete picture of all the pockets of cultural expression, such as local games, regional foods, craft traditions or distinctive styles of music.

"At the root, I'm looking for points of origin or creative centers. That's truly my fundamental interest. And I've learned it can be a single neighborhood like Frenchtown or Liberty Road or the

Fourth Ward here in Houston. This work was in a way inspired by that long-ago meeting with Henry Thomas."

Thomas—one of dozens of Southern blacks to record with companies eager to tap the so-called "race" market of the 1920s—was important for two reasons.

First, already a middle-aged man at the time of his recording debut, he was one of the oldest musicians to record. His repertoire was a grab bag of nineteenth-century black musical traditions. He was something of a musical time machine, bringing to life what had hitherto been dry notations of early, amateur musicologists. In addition to the blues that were so popular at the time, Thomas performed religious songs, dance numbers, minstrel-influenced pieces and travel songs—whimsically mixing verses from one song with those of another in what must have been a mirror of his live performances.

Second, Thomas was one of the few black musicians—if not the only—to spice his commercial recordings with the quills, or panpipes. This folk instrument consisted of a series of bamboo tubes of differing lengths and pitches.

By the time McCormick met the man, he had abandoned the quills for his metal whistle. An impromptu, documentary recording session the next day reaffirmed Thomas was pathetically past his prime.

McCormick has never released what probably was the old musician's last recording session. The results of the performance lie in a tangled jumble of recording wire—the forerunner of magnetic recording tape—in a Houston attic.

Years later, McCormick returned to his Thomas research. Using clues from Thomas's songs—place names of Texas & Pacific railroad stops from a travel song, for instance—he was successful in finding people who had known or thought they had known Thomas decades earlier.

The results of McCormick's undertaking, along with reflections on Thomas's significance and analysis of his songs, were included in the notes of a 1976 reissue of Thomas' known recorded output ("Henry Thomas," *Ragtime Texas*, Herwin 209).

Similarly, McCormick has pioneered research regarding Houston's Santa Fe group of pianists.

The group of musicians, dozens of them, most of whom never recorded, took its name from the railroad that provided a favorite means of transportation. And, invariably, they would respond when asked the name of a song—just about any song—"That's the Santa Fe."

Robert Shaw, a Stafford native who later moved to Austin, is perhaps the best known of the group, having been extensively recorded by McCormick in 1965. But even Shaw admitted his artistry was eclipsed by musicians such as Harold Holliday, who performed as "Black Boy Shine."

The Santa Fe group reflected a distinctive Fourth Ward art form. Shaw and another Fourth Ward pianist, Buster Pickens, astounded McCormick by consistently identifying the pianist and his ward of origin when they were played rare, old recordings of barrelhouse piano.

"They would only have to hear a few notes, just a touch of the piano, that's how distinctive it was," McCormick said.

The song "Ma Grinder" was the group's test piece, the ultimate measure of a pianist's skill, McCormick said. Training for the musicians began early, and neighborhood children would gather on the front porch of a Fourth Ward Italian grocery, where the proprietor had provided them with a piano, to match their skills. "Each would play a version of the song distinctively his own," McCormick said. And thus the tradition grew.

The songs are fraught with Fourth Ward references. "Dog House Blues" commemorates an establishment on West Dallas Street that provided a haven for down-on-their-luck musicians. The proprietor of the bar would even cook rabbits snared by musicians in nearby vacant lots. Holliday roamed through the Sugar Land area, and his "Brown House Blues" memorializes a brothel in Richmond's "Mud Alley."

Even though members of the group had long since dispersed—Shaw to Austin, Rob Cooper and others to parts unknown—Pickens became the Santa Fe historian. "He became a historian, a source," McCormick said. "He became passionate about learning things he had forgotten about."

Shaw died earlier this year in Austin. Pickens was killed some years ago in a quarrel over twenty-five cents. "His cousin shot him with a .22," McCormick said.

McCormick met Hopkins, the hard-drinking, lyrically inventive Houston bluesman, in 1954 through the auspices of—oddly enough—his mother. She was working as an X-ray technician at the Telephone Road office of a doctor whose patients included Bill Quinn—the owner of Gold Star Records, Hopkins' label at the moment.

Much of Hopkins' finest work was waxed for Gold Star; and when McCormick watched the musician at work, he was struck by a realization: "He was essentially making a sound photograph."

Hopkins' blues were brooding, frequently autobiographical and topical. A space shot was commemorated as "Happy for John Glenn Blues," and a bitter cold spell found expression in January 1961 as "Ice Storm Blues."

In the latter, a droll account of the worst winter storm in thirty-eight years, Hopkins observes—to the spare accompaniment of drums and his guitar—"You know it's bad weather here in Houston. You know it's about to get everybody down."

Hopkins then versifies on visiting a used car lot only to be told all the autos have "busted blocks."

Then he continues:

If you can't get there by water, you can't get there by land.
I was in Galveston one day, when they were picking fishes up
with their hands.
You know it was an awful freeze when a fish gives up the ghost.
He used to jump and dip and dodge from me in the water,
And he didn't try that prank no more.

Until his association with McCormick, who recorded him in
1959, Hopkins' fame was confined largely to the black community. He had recorded duets with Fifth Ward pianist "Thunder"
Smith on the California-based Aladdin label as early as 1946. But
his club dates were casual appearances in neighborhood bars,
and his day jobs frequently consisted of playing and singing on
the Dowling Street bus.

By the late 1950s, McCormick was hosting Monday-night folk
music programs at the Alley Theater. And Hopkins' debut under-
scored the cultural gap between blacks and whites. "I hadn't announced that Hopkins would perform," McCormick said, "because
I wasn't sure I would be able to get him.

"I introduced him as a musician who played his guitar walking
up and down Dowling Street, and at a key phrase, he was to
begin playing. I said the phrase, and he began 'I been hoboing,
hoboing.'" The audience, mesmerized, responded with silent attention—a disconcerting development for a musician accustomed
to the irreverent audience participation of a beer hall.

"A preacher sure doesn't get much 'amen' in this church,"
Hopkins sniffed between verses.

"I didn't then understand what he was saying," McCormick
said, "but he'd identified a basic cultural division." A black audience, McCormick said, would have urged him on, exhorted him
to greater musical heights. Even though the audience gave him an

Lightnin Hopkins.
Houston Chronicle photo.

Robert Shaw.
Houston Chronicle photo.

Mance Lipscomb.
Houston Chronicle photo.

ovation at the end of the song, applause simply wasn't the appreciation to which he was accustomed, McCormick said.

Hopkins, born in Centerville in 1912, frequently performed on Houston streets in the 1940s and 1950s with an older man, Leona-born vocalist Alger "Texas" Alexander.

Like Thomas, Alexander's repertoire was filled with "pre-blues" numbers, many of them drawn from prison and work-song traditions. "Texas Alexander was unique," McCormick said. "There was no other artist like him on record. He represents one of the most basic of blues singers. He moans and sings his songs like an ancient field holler."

Alexander served time in prison—some say for the murder of his wife—and his evil reputation likely enhanced his stature as a bluesman. Bluesmen, after all, were purveyors of the devil's music. "He probably circulated the rumor himself," McCormick said.

Again like Thomas, Alexander's songs were filled with references to local events and people. "One of the most personal songs deals with a bunch of guys being chased by a constable. The chase is described in detail, including its end. I think there was an accident with a car knocking down a light post. It would be an utterly meaningless song outside a relatively small area of East Texas."

Alexander's recorded output—available now on a Dutch label—includes some of the most sexually explicit blues ever commercially recorded. "Some of his songs are as filthy as the blues get," said McCormick.

Prison work songs—as heard in Alexander's recordings—represent one of the oldest, richest veins of black music. "A recording of a work song is just a sample," McCormick said. "It might actually last an hour, ranging over a wide number of topics. Often the lines, by implication, are religious. There might be interjections of 'Can I get a witness?' But a song that begins talking about hammering on a church building might end up being about 'hammering on my baby.'"

Prison work songs, which relieve tedium and set the pace for work, attracted the interest of the father-son team of folklorists John A. and Alan Lomax more than fifty years ago. The results of the Lomax field work, issued by the Library of Congress, were fascinating, but the sound quality often was poor. In 1965, McCormick recorded an updated album of Texas prison work songs and prepared to take a group of ex-prisoners to the Newport Folk Festival.

While auditioning performers at a Houston halfway house, McCormick met a man named R. G. Williams, "the toughest man I've met in my life."

Williams' nickname was "Forty," a wry nod to the forty years he was to serve in prison for burglary. "He had been a building tender for ten years, and that's a position in which you have a life expectancy of eight months," McCormick said.

"Forty" quickly whipped the vocal quintet into shape.

The effort to bring raw prison work songs to a folk audience, though, was only marginally successful. The audience was restless, and the performers were terrified.

"I tried to help them anticipate what they would be faced with onstage," McCormick said. "But when they were onstage, in front of the trough they were to use with their hoes, it all fell apart. The hoes went up, they saw that huge audience, and the hoes came down every which way."

McCormick has long since lost track of the group's members.

"'Forty' wasn't like the others," he said. "He had a plan; he was determined to clean up his act. He had a brother working in an auto plant in Flint, Michigan, and he was going up there. He wasn't going to do any more time.

"I know he got to Flint, but I never found out what became of him. You often wonder about things like that."

Working Hard, Joking Hard on the Frontier

=========== **Lawrence Clayton**

Dallas Times Herald
Sunday, August 21, 1983

Life on the American Western frontier required physical stamina, but it also demanded psychological toughness to wrest a living from a harsh land far from familiar surroundings. Part of this psychological "edge" was provided by humor, and no gentle thing was this kind of fun.

Often the humor was found in rough and tumble practical jokes and outrageous bragging. Gentleness did not fit into that era. At first glance, it seems a little surprising that in a situation where life was uncertain already, this abusive and dangerous kind of humor would be practiced. In Owen Wister's *Virginian*, however, the title character, in addition to being an outstanding cowboy, was quite a prankster. Such was life then.

One way the frontier folk had of reminding themselves of their toughness and resiliency was singing songs that recount in humorous ways situations in which individuals pull practical jokes and brag of their promises. Some of these songs, which make up part of the body of songs collected by John Lomax and published in one of three editions of *Cowboy Songs and Other Frontier Ballads* (1910, 1916, 1938), remind us not only that danger was ever

present, but that the people, in reminding themselves of examples of it, seemed to entertain themselves and effect a catharsis of their fears of such a situation by laughing at danger.

It is safe to say that the newcomer or "greenhorn" was held in disdain and often was treated inhumanely on the frontier. This treatment served to initiate the tenderfoot to the dangers of the new life and perhaps prepared him to cope with adversity much as boot camp does for Marine recruits. One of the tricks commonly played on the greenhorns was putting one on a horse unaccustomed, if not downright hostile, to riders. I can recall my grandfather chuckling about instances of doing this even in fairly contemporary times.

Two songs, "The Zebra Dun," and "The Skew-Ball Black," involve this type of incident. In the first song a stranger drifts into a cow camp and relates some of his experiences while serving on a fighting ship at sea, tales the cowboys could hardly believe because of their limited experience. The traveler then asks to borrow a horse to continue his journey. Hoping to put the stranger in his place, the jealous men eagerly select a known outlaw. To their surprise, "The stranger sat upon [the wildly bucking horse] and curled his black mustache/ Just like a summer boarder waiting for his hash." In this case the joke backfires on the pranksters, and the stranger wins respect because he obviously already is initiated into the cowboy life.

In "The Skew-Ball Black," the trick succeeds in showing up a greenhorn for what he is. A young man aspiring to become a cowboy comes to Texas and is quickly tested by ranch hands on the spread where he intends to work. When the horse the men saddle for him begins to pitch, the reaction is predictable: "They rolled and tumbled and yelled . . . /For [the horse] threw me a-whirling all over the sod." Instead of sympathy, the initiate finds derision: "I went to the boss and I told him I'd resign/ The fool tumbled over [in laughter], and I thought he was dying." Here the young man is derided for his inability to stay on the bucking horse and also learns a lesson for himself and for the listeners of the song about how demanding life on the frontier is.

A similar risk resulting in a dangerous situation is "Jess's Dilemma." Jess, the hero of the song, gets bored one night on guard and decides to rope a calf "for some fun, that was all." The unexpected result is the stampeding of the herd. Once the situation settles down, the crew accepts the incident in good spirit. But this song serves as a warning to others to avoid this kind of fun.

Practical jokes were only one element of this kind of humor. Another involves bragging, a practice designed to raise one's opinion of himself and to impress others, even if artificially. The Western braggart is seen in several pieces in Lomax's collection. Characteristic of this kind of song is "The Desperado," which depicts the braggart, obviously the ring-tailed roarer of folklore fame, in all his glory. The speaker characterizes himself as "a howler from the prairies of the West." He claims, "If you want to die with terror, look at me," and continues by saying, "I'm chain-lightning," and "I'm the snorter of the boundless prairie." The chorus, apparently sung by an appreciative audience, sums up the view the man wants to project: "He's a killer and a hater. He's the great annihilator. He's a terror of the boundless prairie." Why anyone would want to be depicted in that way may seem strange, unless he is drunk. This one may be, or perhaps he just wants to convince himself that he is tough enough to face adversity and survive, even thrive.

The difficult day-to-day homelife in the West also draws comment apparently designed to reinforce the fortitude of both men and women. A vivid description is found in "The Texian Boys," also called "Mississippi Girls" and sometimes "Louisiana Girls." That this song was in the cowboy's repertoire suggests the enjoyment they found in depicting the primitive conditions in early Texas. The following version I collected in 1978 from a then 102-year-old blind and almost deaf woman in an Abilene nursing home. Her version differs somewhat from Lomax's longer one, but here is Minnie Young's rendition of the song:

Come all you Missouri girls and listen to my noise
Mind how you court those Texas boys
For if you do, your portion it will be
Cold Johnny cake and venison is all you'll see.

They'll take you up on a black jack hill,
And there they will leave you so much against your will
In a piece long house and a puncheon floor
Sandrock chimney and a rawhide door
Sandrock chimney and a rawhide door.

When they milk, they milk in a gourd
Strain it in the corner and cover it with a board

Some gets a little, and some gets none
That is the way the Texians run
That is the way the Texians run.

Mrs. Young learned this song in Kentucky in the late 1890s and could still smile about it more than eighty years later, because she moved to Texas as a young woman at the turn of the century and certainly proved herself a survivor.

The songs discussed here, as well as numerous others in the various collections of such songs, provide evidence of the humor of physical abuse and danger on the frontier, and they contain as well a feeling that the proper mental attitude reinforced by humor perceived in these situations and bragging about the ability to handle this kind of life helped people cope with a demanding existence.

Cow Chip Tea

Haywood Hygh

Marshall News Messenger
February 15, 1998

In the late thirties and early forties the cold, flu, and pneumonia viruses were on the rampage in the communities of East Texas, northern Louisiana, and the southern tip of Arkansas. The viruses were perhaps worse than they had ever been before. The principal medicines used during that period were those made from herbs, better known as folk medicines. Most of them proved to be unequal to the occasion. The death rate during the cold and flu season (from sometime in September up until the last of February) increased to a remarkable extent.

The sure remedy for these viruses was cow chip tea (a tea made from cow dung). Yes, cow chip tea! Nobody knows exactly when it all started or who came up with this timely discovery. Nonetheless, the news about it spread like a wildfire. When the rural Negroes found out that cow chip tea was the magic bullet, so to say, almost everybody jumped on the bandwagon. When the local folk healers (unlettered root doctors, the only doctors most of the rural Negroes saw and could afford for medical treatment) heard the good news about cow chip tea, they too started making it, using the product to enhance their business in the local communities. Having lived in the communities all of their lives, the folk healers were already knowledgeable of their patients' social and religious predilections. And in the parlance of time, the rural and a goodly number of the urban folks believed in them. "If Doc says it's alright, that it's a sho' cuo' (cure) ya, then it has to be alright."

I recall vividly that the sale of cow chip tea almost outsold Garrett Snuff and Hadacol. Hadacol was a patent tonic invented by Dudley Le Blanc, a native of Louisiana. The tonic was very popular in the rural and urban South in the 1940s and 1950s. It became one of the most sought-after iron and vitamin tonics of the twentieth century. Most of the folks who took the medicine thought it to be a god-sent, cure-all formula.

The root doctors doctored up their product with corn whiskey to enhance its potency. They advertised their product on the sides of their wagons, cars, and pickup trucks during the cold and flu season.

Cow Chip Tea, The Medicine of the Future
A Sure Remedy for Colds, Flu, and Pneumonia Viruses

The self-appointed doctors would encourage potential customers by telling them about all the folks they had already "cuoed. . . . Folks who were at death's doh. I pushed the tombstone right off of their heads!" Of course the names mentioned were purported to be persons who lived in another county, "ovah" in Caddo Parish, Louisiana or Marion County, Texas. The potential customers had no way of knowing whether or not the doctor was being truthful with them, as they did little traveling outside their own communities.

Our doctor, Dr. Whitehead, was from Marion County (Jefferson). He had a large clientele over in the northeastern section of Harrison County (Marshall), especially in the communities of Baldwin,

Woodlawn, Karnack, Leigh, and Uncertain (Caddo Lake area). Lord, the Negroes who lived in these communities thought that he was some kind of black Jesus! He was a lanky man of dark complexion. His long, gray hair was straggly. Slightly osteoporotic, he walked slowly and ungainly. Furthermore, he had a speech impediment. I had read so much about Moses in my Sunday School classes, that in my childhood fantasy, I imagined Dr. Whitehead to be the very spirit and image of Moses. His faded white shirt was grimy from being washed in water fetched from Black Cypress Bayou. He wore the same blue serge suit and wrinkled bow-tie year in and year out. The suit was almost as slick as glass. Mama used to say that it needed to be cleaned as badly as a dead man needed a coffin. Bless my soul to heaven and back, he talked so slowly that one could almost catnap while he finished a sentence. His medical vocabulary was similar to his regular vocabulary: very limited. What's more, his method of examining his patient was so unorthodox. The patient was simply asked to stick out his/her tongue. The moment he saw the patient's tongue, Dr. Whitehead knew exactly what ailed him/her.

"Tox-tox-tox-tox-ci-ci-ci-ty!" he would bellow out in a bluffing tone of voice. "Great great day in the morn-morn-morn-in', poison from that dat-dat-datblame virus done spread all o-o-ovah yoh body, by-jingle!"

The reluctant patient, already weakened by the cold or flu virus, squirmed nervously in the split-bottomed chair, gaped in utter disbelief, adding to the doctor's travail. Most of them didn't even know the meaning of the word toxicity. If he were trying to scare the living hell out of them, I should think that he succeeded. At this point the patient was willing to invest four bits in a quart of the doctor's cow chip tea.

There were any number of disputes, though they were never violent ones, about who should make and distribute the newfound formula. The local practitioners were of the persuasion that they had experimented with the formula, ironed out all the bugs, and proved to the folks that it was sure-cure for the cold, flu, and pneumonia viruses. What's more, they had taught the folk healers how to make the stuff, with one exception: the local practitioners didn't lace their formula with white lightning. The uncelebrated practitioners wanted some dignity, some recognition for their all-important contribution to the science of medicine.

On the other hand, the smart aleck root doctors were seasoned politicians. Their rhetoric took on a religious fervor. Having eclipsed the practitioners at the market place, the root doctors steadfastly maintained that they had been preordained by God to heal the sick; that they were bearers of good news. After watching his people suffering and dying from the several viruses, God had at last responded to their humble supplications. His spirit had directed them to one of nature's greatest healing sources: the lowly cow dung!

To a large degree, the good news about the cow chip tea formula was spread by the root doctors, for they had means of transportation.

Papa was among the best herbalist of that era. He was bequeathed this invaluable knowledge from his father, a long line of African ancestors, and the Caddo Indians. He knew too well that the root doctors who had started making and selling cow chip tea tonics were pulling the wool over the folks' eyes, but he dared not tell them the truth about the sacred cows.

Papa didn't like the tea made by the root doctors. So, he made the tea for members of his own family and close relatives. A vigorously religious man, Papa resolved not to lace his tea with white lightning. His concoction was composed of cow dung, dried leaves from ginseng plants (it has the equivalency and similar effect of marijuana), and mullen leaves, etc. The cow dung, along with a smidgen of clay dirt, was wrapped in a piece of cloth. He stated that the clay dirt aided in the purification of the cow dung. The older the chips were, the better they were. Additionally, Papa added small portions of his secret herbs. These herbs led to the final perfection of the tea. These ingredients were mixed up and put in a pot. Having boiled for approximately thirty minutes, the formula was poured into another pot. It was then laced with either muscadine or grape wine, vintages usually reserved for the Holy Sacrament and Christmas and New Years toasts.

When I was a boy, Papa took me to the forest and pointed out any number of these herbs to me. However, the years passed, and by and by I left home for the Army in 1949. Shortly before he died in 1979, Papa again told me the names of the herbs. Enfeebled by a long spell of illness, he was unable to return to the forest again with me and point them out.

As I grew older, I realized that it was either the whiskey or the wine and ginseng weeds that made the tea patient friendly, regardless of whether it was made by the practitioners or the root doctors. I fondly remember the happy faces of those patients who had just had a half cup of lukewarm tea. They looked like they had been spaced out. A few moments later they were fast asleep. I am told that numerous persons claimed that not only did the tea cure their viruses, but it also increased their sexual awareness.

There was at least one saving grace. As far as I can remember, there were no deaths linked to cow chip tea. Regardless of its popularity among the folks who lived in the rural and urban communities, cow chip tea remained in disrepute with the medical profession, which was helpless, however, to impede its acceptance by the masses who could not afford medical care.

The coming of World War II ushered in a new era. The opportunities for education and social progress for Negroes throughout the South were unprecedented. During the early 1940s the PWA (Public Works Administration) built two schools in the community of Karnack, one for the colored students and one for the white students. The Negroes named their school George Washington

Carver High School, for grades one through twelve. The George Washington Carver High School's 1944 graduating class motto, "No Victory Without Labor," became a positive resolve for the several communities that made up the George Washington Carver School District.

Nevertheless, during the same period of time, momentum was building up for a confrontation between the small Negro middle class and the masses who tried desperately to hold on to their traditional mores. The small Negro middle class, considered to be "highfalutin and uppity" by the masses, consisted of mostly teachers, doctors, and preachers. As their ranks grew in numbers, they distanced themselves from those persons who sought the medical advice of root doctors and those practitioners who peddled cow chip tea. When I was in the seventh grade, a young lady who sat next to me in class asked our teacher what she thought about cow chip tea. Our teacher, a young lady who grew up in the community and attended Bishop College, refused to respond, sitting there like someone had sealed her lips with crazy glue.

Deeply worried about some of the counterproductive things he saw taking place in the community, Professor Rufus B. Anderson, the principal at George Washington Carver High School, asked Dr. F. E. Williams to come down to Karnack and talk to the citizens about the medical benefits of cow chip tea used in the treatment of cold, flu, and pneumonia viruses. In addition to his practice in Marshall, Dr. Williams also had a clinic in the community of Leigh, only five miles away from Karnack.

Dr. Williams eagerly accepted Professor Anderson's invitation. The school gymnasium (also used as an auditorium) was filled to its capacity.

Speaking urgently, Dr. Williams began by telling his seemingly receptive audience that as far as he knew, there was no scientific data among those who worked in the medical profession that validated the claims of healing of cow chip tea. Furthermore, cow chip tea was an illegal product, one that had not been approved as medicine by the U. S. Food and Drug Administration. He assured them that if there were any benefit at all, it was no more than a placebo effect. Even worse, the notion of drinking a tea made from cow dung was unsanitary and thoroughly disgusting.

There was stunned silence as he spoke. His speech earned him hatred of those who saw cow chip tea as a present-day panacea, one that was sent down from heaven by God. For the most part, his warning did little to persuade his audience to stop using the formula. The folks were still deeply rooted in folkways. The African ancestral bond between the community, lay persons, and folk healers was still very strong.

There was one minor disturbance during the time Dr. Williams was speaking. It was so genuine that the audience became disconcerted by it. The person making the "quack, quack, quack" sound sat only a short distance from where I sat. I should think that Walt Disney would have loved his duck rendition. Later, I learned that the "quack, quack, quacking" was directed to the speaker, Dr. Williams, meaning that he was not a good doctor.

I didn't know the man. Two gentlemen who sat next to me spoke quietly among themselves. It was said in my hearing that the quacking man was one of the bootleggers who distilled the corn whiskey used to enhance the quality of the root doctors' cow chip formula.

The football coach and assistant coach came over to where we sat, beckoning to the gentlemen. He obeyed. Assisted by the coaches, he continued to mimic a duck as he wobbled his way toward the door. The disapproval boos resonated above the weak applause for him.

There were uncounted folktales made up about cow chip tea. The front of the courthouse in Marshall was one of the favorite gathering places for Negroes on Saturdays. The stone-faced statues of the confederate sentinels that guarded the courthouse seemed to have been mindful of their presence. The storytellers became the center of attraction. They were very hospitable. Before beginning the tale, the storyteller would say, "Now, this is the truth, evah I tol' it." Or "If I'm lyin' I'm flyin', and y'all know I don't have no damn wings."

One of the most memorable tales I heard was told by two storytellers. Of course they made it appear as if their meeting up there on this particular day was a coincidence. The tale is about two men. Both of them had daughters who had been quite ill with one of the flu or cold viruses.

"You know, one of my gals was so sick with that datblame flu back heah in April that she couldn't hoe cotton a lick," the first story-teller said. "O' Doc Peterson come ovah and give her some of that cow chip tea. Now, she can out hoe anybody in the family."

The second storyteller giggled, added his lines. "Yeah, one of my gals had it too . . . very bad. O' Doc Peterson come ovah and give her some of that cow chip tea. Now, she's the biggest hoe in town!"

The crowd laughed hilariously and applauded the storytellers, everyone except Papa. An old hope-to-die Baptist preacher, he had no affinity for such mundane entertainment, and refused to validate it. For he felt it reflected badly upon the Negro community.

One of the most celebrated tales from the community of Karnack is the one told about Mr. T. G. Tyler (everybody called him Cap'n for short). Mr. Tyler owned a large general store in the community. Well, rumors had it that the white folks felt that more of them were dying of flu and pneumonia than Negroes. Naturally, they felt that this was an act of discrimination. Reproaching God, however, would have been down right blasphemous. The blame had to be placed upon someone; there had to be an explanation. The Negroes were the only persons whom they could turn to for a plausible explanation. After all, it was their numbers diminishing at a slower rate than whites.

Well, it was not an easy task. As a matter of fact, it was somewhat embarrassing. But the white folks felt they were entitled to know why the good Lord chose to diminish their numbers at a faster rate than coloreds. Too, they had heard nasty rumors about cow chip tea.

The task of looking into the matter was assigned to Mr. T. G. Tyler. The obligation fell to him because a large number of the Negroes in the community lived on his land, shopped at his general store, buying everything from a box of Garrett Snuff to a pine box coffin to bury their dead. Surely, they wouldn't object to his inquiring, for he had always exercised friendship toward them during those dreadful winter months when they were constantly visited upon by the cold, flu, and pneumonia viruses.

Cap'n had it all figured out. There was a young colored fellow who worked for him as a truck driver-chauffeur. Everybody called the big, ebony complexioned fellow Malinke C. So, Malinke C. was driving Cap'n to work. The sniffles were biting at Cap'n's nose on this particular morning. Surely, he was coming down with the flu virus or something. The time was ripe; he popped the question to Malinke C.

"Huh, Bo" (his pet word for almost everybody), he said, blotting his nose. "It seems like we have more white folks dying of the flu and pneumonia than colored folks. What kind of medicine are you all taking for these viruses?"

Well, Malinke C. didn't have anything to hide; he spoke forthrightly. "Well, Cap'n," he said, driving slowly. "Colored folks are taking cow chip tea. If you start taking it in time, it'll cuo' (cure) ya' evah time. . . . Yes-suh-ree!"

How disgusting, Mr. Tyler thought. He didn't want to believe what he was hearing. He too had heard rumors, but he just couldn't believe that anyone in his/her right mind would resort to drinking a tea made from cow dung. He felt feverish and began to sneeze profusely. The more he thought about the matter, the more he was inclined to try it. After all, it cured the colored folks; it even made some of them fat. And whatever the medicines were that the doctors up in Marshall had prescribed for all of the white folks didn't seem to be doing any good. He had a change of heart about the matter. "Got dahg it," he would chance it!

Malinke C. drove up in front of the store and stopped.

Cap'n got out the car, leaned over on the side of the door. "Well, Bo," Cap'n said. "I want you to go on back to the house, go out in the pasture, get some cow chips, and make a tea for me."

"Yah-suh," Malinke C. said. "I'll be too glad to do that for you, Cap'n."

"Uh," Cap'n grunted, "you'd better bring me a little piece back down here to the store so I can be chewing on it until the tea is ready."

Post Notes

Even when I was a boy, I had my doubts about the healing benefits of cow chip tea. However, I didn't develop a healthy disdain for it as I did castor oil. But Papa was the man! He would set the cup on the table, sit in front of me, and say, "Bottom up!" So I drank. For sure, the ginseng leaves and wine gave it a palatable taste. A few minutes after I had drunk the stuff, I felt pretty good, a little tipsy I should say. I am not sure that medical considerations were served.

That is all history now. Nevertheless, the events of that period still resonate in the back of my mind today. As a fledgling, the events nurtured and enlarged my life. Undeniably, there was diversity as usual, but the strong fibers of the folkway bond held rural-dominated communities together.

I have come to believe that we all share a reciprocal responsibility to evaluate diversity, though controversial it might well be. We cannot avoid contact with certain attitudes which prevail within our midst, nor can we live within a world of ideas unto ourselves.

I knew most of the people mentioned here (most of them are now deceased), and I have an abiding affection for and fond memories of those persons. Each one of them acted and spoke to his/her own personal experience.

Orient Hotel Saw Good Times and Bad

Elmer Kelton

West Texas Livestock Weekly
March 12, 1970

PECOS—When the Orient Hotel was built at the corner of First and Cedar Street here in 1904, it was considered the finest hostelry on the Texas Pacific Railroad between Fort Worth and El Paso. It was a three-story extension on an eight-year-old two-story red sandstone building known in those days as the Number 11 Saloon.

It was in that saloon that one of the Pecos' most famous shootouts had taken place in 1896.

But passage of time and the building of more modern hotels and motels eventually put the Orient in the shade. There was even a time, after several changes of name and ownership and late in its hotel career, when the Orient's once respectable halls began carrying a whispered reputation regarding commerce of an ancient but embarrassing nature. For a time it was closed entirely.

It is open again now, restored to much of its original condition, regarded in its day as minor splendor. But its modern mission is as a museum, displaying and preserving some of the flavor and artifacts of Pecos's growing-up days as a rough-and-ready cowtown. Aside from the importance of preserving these things, the museum may have served another timely and useful purpose: giving a divided community a project that helped pull people together after one of Pecos's most trying ordeals: the Billie Sol Estes disaster.

Pecos itself is much older than the hotel, having started as a railroad station when the TP tracks bridged to the west bank of the Pecos River in 1881. In its early days it was commonly called Pecos City and had a reputation as a cowboy's town, rough but fair, playful but firm. It was a center of commerce for ranch country several days' horseback ride in all directions. It became home in his final years for retired gunfighter Clay Allison, who came to town for an occasional spree but otherwise stayed close to his ranch upriver.

It was home for Sheriff Bud Frazer and gunman Jim Miller, who shot at each other on the streets of Pecos more than once, their feud ending at the neighboring town of Toyah one September day in 1896, when Miller carried a shotgun into a saloon where Frazer was engaged in a quiet game of seven-up and calmly blasted Frazer out of his chair. Miller died beneath a barn rafter in Ada, Oklahoma, of what in those days was simply known as "throat trouble."

But back to the hotel. R. S. Johnson, a former Texas Ranger, bought the corner property in 1896 and put up a two-story saloon-hotel building of red stone quarried from the other side of the river near Barstow. The new paint smell had hardly gotten out of the place when Barney Riggs, noted Pecos country rancher and gunfighter, got word that a couple of toughs were coming down from Carlsbad to see if he was as good as his reputation. They walked into the saloon as he stood at the bar, one pausing at the door, the other approaching Riggs.

They found out his reputation was justified, but they never lived long enough to ponder on it. Brass plates on the floor of the restored saloon show where the two died.

Pecos folks eventually tired of the free-and-easy days of old, and the violence that was part and parcel of it. In 1906 a local-option election voted out all the saloons, and the Number 11 along with all the others was given a year to clean out its stock and change trade.

By then, however, Johnson had built the large adjacent hotel building to provide a first class hostelry just a few steps from the TP depot, and the saloon was secondary anyway. It was a pool hall for awhile, then was leased out and partitioned for offices. Upstairs, the older hotel rooms were connected to the new ones by a corridor. Furniture was bought in Chicago. Each room had a big rug, an iron bedstead, two chairs, a dresser and mirror, and a washstand with large bowl and pitcher. None of the rooms had a private bath, but a washstand was provided on the ground floor and one large complete bathroom on each of the other two floors. An artesian well drilled behind the hotel had enough pressure behind it to lift water to the third floor. Carbide gas lamps lighted the building.

Though it was a short stroll across to the depot, the hotel nevertheless maintained a big black hack, driven by a Negro and pulled by white horses, which met all trains and hauled drummers and other customers across to the hotel so they didn't have to step into the dust or mud (a lot more dust than mud at Pecos in those days, as now). The hotel maintained a sample room so the drummers could set up their displays; merchants came down to the hotel to see them.

Family style meals were served in the large dining room, drawing a lot of trade besides the people who stayed in the hotel.

But time went on, the traveling public got wheels of its own and began to depend much less upon the railroad. As railroad traffic declined, so did the hotel.

The hotel was not operating in the late 1950s and early 1960s but Billie Sol Estes was. Upon the collapse of his financial empire in 1962, pulling down many Pecos businesses and a great many individual businessmen and farmers with it, Pecos went through one of its most trying periods. A great deal of factionalism arose, and many longtime friends found relationships badly strained.

A little before this time, late rancher Louis Roberson had begun to talk to Barney Hubbs about a Pecos museum. The Orient Hotel was one of the few old buildings still left that seemed right to house the type of collections Roberson envisioned. One thing led to another, and the city optioned the building, turning it over to a newly formed West of the Pecos Museum group in 1962.

Restoring the old building took a lot of time, money and donated work. It provided a common interest and meeting ground for many people who had been pulled apart by the stresses and strains of Pecos's own private recession. In its own way, it helped heal over some of the wounds.

Today a number of widely varied clubs and organizations sponsor their own individual museum projects. For instance, the medical society put in the Dr. Jim Camp Room, which is set up to show

how a typical country doctor's office and treatment room looked in horse and buggy days, complete with the tools of his trade. The Modern Study Club restored the bridal suite to its original romantic condition. The Rock and Gem Club maintains a permanent display. The Merry Wives Club set up a typical turn-of-the-century kitchen and dining room. Many of these organizations meet regularly in the museum building.

Some of the rooms are yet to be restored; a lot of work is still ahead. The third story remains unused, says Mrs. Fay Duncan, museum hostess. She admits she despaired a dozen times when the restoration work first began, the modern false ceilings removed to show the original old high ones, and the many coats of paint removed from the oak woodwork of the hotel lobby to reveal delicate hand carving that had been forgotten for decades. Last year the museum counted 14,000 visitors.

There is still a little local controversy over the bar in the restored saloon. It was found in an old building in Monahans. A considerable amount of evidence indicates it is the original one where Barney Riggs stood when the two Carlsbad men came to call him out, but no one can be altogether sure. So local residents can only adapt the late J. Frank Dobie's philosophy regarding a good story: "If it didn't happen just that way, it should have."

El Ojo and Other Folk Beliefs

Joe Graham

The Fort Worth Star-Telegram
Friday, June 8, 1984

All of us have them.

They guide us in times of uncertainty. They provide us with explanations for the otherwise inexplicable. They give us hope when others say there is none. They help us order the world with its myriad of facts and experiences into a manageable, familiar, comfortable whole.

They are our folk beliefs.

They are usually called superstitions, a pejorative label which we normally apply to the folk beliefs of others. What we know, we know. What someone else "knows," especially if it differs from what we KNOW, we label superstition.

In the words of Dr. John O. West, folklorist at the University of Texas at El Paso, "Superstition is what some other damn fool believes."

Simply put, folk beliefs are those beliefs which are passed on orally from one person to another and from one generation to another, through time and space. It is passed on without the sanctions of such official institutions as schools, churches or professional societies.

Once a belief becomes a part of the official institution's accepted doctrines or beliefs, usually set in print, it is no longer subject to the processes which make it a folk belief.

For example, there is official religion and folk religion. Roman Catholics believe in saints canonized and recognized by the church. This is official religion. It remains relatively unchanged for centuries. Many Mexicans and Mexican Americans also believe in folk saints—those who have not been canonized by the church: San Lorenzo, for example, and, according to Professor Octavio Romanio-I, Don Pedrito Jaramillo of South Texas, a well-known *curandero*, or folk healer, whose reputation has spread throughout the Southwest and Mexico. He has a shrine built in his honor near Falfurrias. Icons of the famous healer can be found in homes throughout South Texas, and beyond. The official Church does not recognize him as a saint, but the folk believe in him and treat him as a saint, official religion notwithstanding.

Folk belief education begins long before one enters school. By the time a person enters school, he has acquired a pretty clear sense of what the world is like and how he fits into that world, called "world-view" by academicians. He learns this from his parents and other family members, as well as his friends and play-mates.

He may discover, as he enters school, that this view of the world is not the official view. He may discover that tarantulas are not deadly poisonous; that eating fish and drinking milk will not make one deathly sick; that giving a knife or pair of scissors to a friend will not sever a friendship; that there is no logical connection between "bad luck" and black cats crossing one's path.

The greater the difference between his world-view and that of official institutions, the greater the dissonance he will experience, the more he will have to acculturate to official culture.

When we hear the folk beliefs of others, particularly a group whose world-view differs from ours, we automatically assume that theirs is wrong and ours is right. Hence, we give them a negative label: superstition. They sound silly to us because we do not understand the premises upon which they are based.

Among the Mexican-American folk beliefs most widely written about, which attract our attention most easily because they differ so much from our own, are the folk beliefs about sickness and healing—folk medical beliefs. We hear that they believe in witches (*brujas*), in the evil eye (*mal de ojo*), "magical fright" (*susto*) and other strange and remarkable illnesses.

Since we may have already stereotyped Mexican Americans as being illogical and "superstitious," we may just assume that this "proves" (validates) our negative stereotype. Further investigation, however, reveals that, given the premises upon which these beliefs are based, both the illnesses and their treatments are perfectly logical.

These premises are based on the world-view of these Mexican Americans who take part in this folk culture—it should be emphasized that not all Mexican Americans believe in the folk medical system: many do not. But for those who share the traditional world-view of their culture, the folk medical system is a coherent, internally logical and consistent set of beliefs and practices which provide theories of illness causes, of appropriate diagnostic procedures, and a set of remedies which at least minimally meet their needs.

Many of these remedies, in fact, are effective. All require faith. Let us turn to an example.

A folk illness syndrome common among those in the traditional culture is *mal de ojo*, or simply *el ojo*. Often glossed by scholars as "evil eye," it has little in common with that malevolent force, at least as the English term implies. It is better thought of as "sickness from looking."

Based on the belief that one individual can influence another without physically touching him, *mal de ojo* is caused by someone with a "strong" or piercing gaze looking at someone or something in excess admiration, resulting in harm.

Children and women are particularly susceptible to *el ojo*. Interestingly, those who cause the illness are not held responsible for it: that is, there are no sanctions taken against the person, so long as he/she is willing to assist in the treatment. If someone believes he has a strong gaze and may be responsible for incidences of *el ojo*, he may neutralize the effect merely by touching the potential victim.

A child with *mal de ojo* will cry for no apparent reason, suffer fever and headaches, lose his appetite, sleep fitfully and become generally listless. The illness can be fatal if not treated. Diagnosis is based principally on the symptoms and may be confirmed during treatment.

There are two basic strategies for treating *el ojo*: take a garment (scarf, shirt, etc.) from the suspected source of the problem (the person with the strong gaze), rub the child with this garment, accompanied by prayers. In addition, just to make sure, the healer may choose to use the egg treatment, particularly if the suspected source is unknown or unavailable to assist.

The child is disrobed, except for his undergarments, and placed on a bed on a clean sheet. The healer takes a fresh egg, one never refrigerated, and rubs it on the child's head, arms and body. The egg is moved in the sign of the cross, accompanied by prayers. When this process is completed, the egg is cracked and poured into a saucer, cup or glass containing water. A small cross of broomstraw is floated on the water. Later, if the egg has formed an "eye" and appears as though it has been cooked, the diagnosis is confirmed and the treatment is complete.

The explanation of the cause and cure is often couched in modern terms: the person who has a "strong" gaze has electricity or magnetism in his eyes, which upsets the balances in the victim's body. The egg absorbs the heat of the fever; consequently, it appears cooked. The use of prayers and the cross, powerful symbols, invoke the faith of devout Catholics.

While we may disagree with the premises upon which this folk medical belief is predicated, we have no trouble following the logic.

Even if we fail to recognize such illnesses as real and the treatments as effective, we should recognize the important function these beliefs serve for those who have often been without the services of modern medical science.

The folk medical system provides a means for naming the illnesses, for diagnosing them, for treating them and for preventing them. These medical beliefs and practices are consonant with the broader world-view. Man can look to God and his servants, the *curanderos*, to help restore and maintain balance and harmony in the universe, as well as the human body.

This folk medical system helps order an important domain in the lives of the believers: that of sickness and health, living and dying. Man has access to powers which permit him to control his destiny, at least to a degree. It gives him a sense of control over elements he could not control otherwise: control over the unknown, the uncertain, even over life and death.

As Mexican Americans move into the mainstream of American life, adopting the official view of the world and of man's role in it, they find it necessary to reject older beliefs. Belief in *brujeria* and *curanderismo* are the first to go; belief in herbal remedies, most readily accepted and explained in terms of official culture, may persist through a lifetime.

Although not a part of that culture, I have a profound respect for the people and their folkways, which have served them and their forebears for many, many generations, since long before medical science evolved.

Even though *el ojo* is not consonant with my understanding of how things work in the world, particularly in the human body, I nevertheless am grateful for the thoughtfulness and concern of those older Mexican-American women who used to come and touch my handsome, very, very blond two-year-old son—just a precaution to prevent harm to a child they admired, perhaps too much.

The Cleo Face

Mike Cox

San Angelo Standard-Times
May 11 and May 18, 1969

One of the prettiest drives in West Texas in the springtime is down Farm to Market Road 2291 from Menard to the post office of Cleo.

But few people but the natives know about Cleo. For one thing, it isn't even on the official Texas Highway Department map of Texas. This seems somewhat out of order, though, because Cleo is the closest town to the birthplace of former Governor Coke Stevenson, who now lives on a ranch near Telephone.

Cleo started out as the Bear Creek community, later became known as Viejo and finally switched to Cleo in 1920, when it was discovered there was a town in Brown County called Viejo. The Bear Creek settlement was about a half-mile off the farm road just outside Cleo. It was settled in the 1850s by Raleigh Gentry, who built a two-room log house and cleared a small farm. In 1862, he sold out to a cattleman named Rance Moore.

Today, the only remnants of the old Gentry ranch are located on property leased by Boyce Hunger. The only visible trace today of the old ranch is a pile of blackened stones, once a fireplace.

"The Cleo Face." Photo by Mike Cox.

Texas Rangers reportedly met up with a cattle rustler they had trailed for some time and killed him in a gun battle near the old cabin.

Mrs. Allen Bishop, a woman interested in local history, is postmaster at Cleo. Her husband runs a small store and gas station.

"When I was a kid," he said, "we had enough boys around here to make up two baseball teams. But the people all moved off and the boys got married and left the country—to make an understatement."

The Cleo school, which still stands, was used until 1936, when the school district consolidated with Junction.

The old Bear Creek Cemetery nearby has about seventy-five graves, one of them belonging to James H. Sewell, who was killed on the Gentry place in 1872 by Indians.

This scenic area also is the site of the "Cleo Face," as local folks put it.

The face is carved on a blackened rock in a pasture leased by Hunger. Though age has made it a bit difficult to see at first glance, a carefully carved, giant-sized face can still be detected on the large stone. The face has a broad nose, glinting eyes and a snarling mouth with long, fang-like teeth.

At first, no one in the area could be found who knew anything about the carving other than the fact that it had been there a long time. Some people said it was carved by Indians, but Texas Indians weren't sculptors. Others theorized the carving represented a bear once seen in the area or depicted the Bear Creek community. Not far away are high rock cliffs and the idea also had been advanced that the stone tumbled down from there.

It didn't take long after a story was published about the mystery face for a solution to come.

About a week later, Mrs. W. E. Allen, Jr., of nearby Junction wrote, saying she knew "a person who can solve the mystery. . . . He is Mr. Frank Patterson, who now lives in Carrizo Springs with his daughter, Mrs. Gene Weaver."

The woman related that Patterson's father bought the land (along Bear Creek where the stone is located) from Rance Moore "and was . . . a tombstone cutter by trade, who carved the stone . . . and many others along that part of Bear Creek while recuperating there from tuberculosis."

Mrs. Chester Bannowsky, wife of a Kimble County rancher and a local historian, provided a little more background.

Moore, she said, was one of the earliest settlers in the area. Patterson's father, N. Q. Patterson, came to Texas with his family in 1868 from Tennessee. The family lived in Limestone and

Williamson counties before finally coming to Kimble County in 1875.

Patterson became one of the leading citizens and was the first county treasurer. Between 1877–78 he was county judge and had served on the first jury in the county in 1876. He married the sister of the last man killed by Indians in Kimble County, Mrs. Bannowsky said.

In 1898, while in New Mexico, the elder Patterson was injured in a horse accident. He died near the mouth of Cox Canyon and was buried near Cloudcroft, New Mexico.

The son of Patterson carved his own niche, incidentally. In 1969, at ninety years of age, he was one of the last remaining old-time West Texas lawmen. But, for a time back in 1918, it didn't look like he was going to make middle age, much less ninety. In fact, on Christmas day, 1918, he was supposed to have been dead.

On that day, he had crossed the muddy Rio Grande southwest of Marfa with a company of Texas Rangers hot on the trail of Mexican banditos. He was left behind in the pursuit and presumed dead. But he really hadn't been left behind. He had, instead, determined to skip up on the bandits himself by using an old Army trail. When he crept up close enough, he opened up on the bandits, exchanging eighteen shots. Reportedly, seven dead bandits later were removed from a hillside they had occupied during the battle.

Patterson, meanwhile, had made a prudent withdrawal. And his captain, J. M. Fox, had left in search of Patterson's body. When the two met up with each other, the captain, having to lead his sorefooted horse by the reins was not pleased with the young Ranger. Angrily, the captain hurled his heavy pistol to the ground, announcing he wasn't going to carry it any farther. Patterson picked it up and still had it in his gun collection fifty years later—a Christmas present on the day he was supposed to have died.

Dr. J. Mason Brewer

James W. Byrd

The Commerce Journal
December 13, 1998

J. Mason Brewer, the first black professor in the English Department at East Texas State University, was hired one year after ETSU hired its first black professor ever, Dr. David Talbot, but Brewer had lectured there at two previous summer folklore symposiums. After the third symposium in 1969, President D. Whitney Halladay (knowing an M.A. thesis had been written about Brewer at ETSU) asked him if he wanted to join the full-time faculty as Distinguished Visiting Professor (since he was above seventy years of age). Brewer agreed. He taught full time at ETSU from September 1969 to January 1975, when he died. That year his biography appeared in *Who's Who in America.*

John Mason Brewer (1896–1975), noted African-American folklorist, son of Minnie T. and J. H. Brewer, was born at Goliad, Texas, near Bahia Mission, on March 24, 1896. Brewer came to ETSU as the state's most prominent black writer and one of the nation's top black folklorists. He had one brother and four schoolteacher sisters. One sister, Dr. Stella Brewer Brooks, a published authority on Joel Chandler Harris and the Uncle Remus tales, shared his interest in folklore. Young Mason attended the segregated public schools of Austin and in 1917 received a B.A. from predominantly black Wiley College in Marshall. Joining the army in 1918, Corporal Brewer spent a year in France, returning to a career as a teacher in the Fort Worth and Dallas school systems. He eventually moved from public schools to black colleges. In 1926, as a professor at Samuel Huston College (now Huston-Tillotson) in Austin, he met University of Texas Professor J. Frank Dobie, who

J. Mason Brewer

influenced his turn from publishing his own poetry to collecting and publishing black folklore. In 1933, he received an M.A. from Indiana University and, in 1951, an honorary doctorate from Paul Quinn College, a private Methodist college then in Waco. Brewer was a Methodist and a Democrat, with political friends as diverse as Governor Allen Shivers and President Lyndon Johnson, whose autographed pictures he displayed.

Brewer's list of "firsts" is impressive. He was the first African-American member of the Texas Folklore Society, addressing its meetings from the 1930s to the 1970s, and publishing in six of its annual volumes. He became the first African-American member of the Texas Institute of Letters in 1954, after being chosen one of the twenty-five best Texas Authors by Theta Sigma Phi, Inc., for *The Word on the Brazos: Negro Preacher Tales from the Brazos Bottoms of Texas*. He was the first African American to serve as vice president of the American Folklore Society. During the Harlem Renaissance of the 1920s, he was one major black writer of his era who stayed in Texas. He eventually became nationally known as a folklorist and popular lecturer, being included in *Who's Who in America* the year he died (1975).

His major books are *The Word on the Brazos* (1954), *Aunt Dicey Tales* (1956), *Dog Ghosts and Other Negro Folk Tales* (1968), put in paperback while he was at ETSU. Of the early volumes of poetry and history, one of each is easily found: *Negrito* (1933) and *Negro Legislators of Texas* (1935) were reprinted in the 1970s. His work makes up a large part of *The Encyclopedia of Black Folklore and Humor,* edited by Henry D. Spalding (1972). Brewer wrote the preface. In 1968, as his last book, he edited the important *American Negro Folklore,* an anthology.

After ten years of out-of-state teaching at Livingston College in North Carolina, Brewer returned to Texas and ended his career at East Texas State University in Commerce, where he was Distinguished Visiting Professor from 1969 until he died at age seventy-eight in January, 1975, from a broken hip. He was buried in Austin, leaving his second wife, Ruth Helen Brewer of Hitchcock, Texas; a son by his first wife, J. Mason Brewer II of Los Angeles, California; one grandson, J. Mason Brewer III; and his brother and sisters.

A biography in the Southwest Writers Series is entitled *J. Mason Brewer: Negro Folklorist* (Austin: Steck-Vaughn, 1967). A short film of his life was made in 1978 by the Texas Folklore Society and the Texas Commission on the Humanities. It is available at the media center at ETSU.

Brewer's international reputation was growing when he died. In 1975, one of the principal Romanian literary journals, *Steaua,* carried a biographical and critical study of Dr. Brewer's work by Dr. Thomas Perry. With it appeared two of his tales translated into Romanian—portraying experiences which readers only a few generations removed from serfdom and acquainted with ethnic confrontations could well understand. Too late, a letter arrived asking him to help edit an anthology of Southwestern American folklore for Romanians.

Dusting Out

━━━━━ Francis Edward Abernethy

Dallas Times Herald
Sunday, November 28, 1982

During the early years of the Depression the Jim Talbots lived in a two-room shack on Grandad's Washita River ranch in the Texas Panhandle. Jim was Grandad's cousin and he helped out on the place and he was peg-legged. He was a big strong man and he wore this regular strap-on peg leg, and I would have given my toy tractor to have seen him take it off and put it on again. As I remember the story—or imagined it—Jim Talbot got caught in the crossfire in a train robbery at a railroad station and stopped the bullet that eventually cost him his leg. That scene is as vivid in my mind now as it was fifty years ago.

Jim's family consisted of Jim and Pearl and their three kids—an older girl and a little boy, and Frances, who was seven years old and my age. Girl that she was, she was the only child to play with for miles and miles of Panhandle plains, and she helped to keep away the high lonesomes that always hung over the prairie. Frances was red-headed and completely freckled and ready to explore the far reaches of any barn or plum thicket or rat's nest. Neither of us could imagine a world without the other, and I loved her dearly.

The Jim Talbots dusted out in 1932. The bottom had already dropped out of the cotton and grain market, and a harvested crop barely paid for the seed. Then the drouth hit. Grandad cut back on his stock and there wasn't any work for Jim and no money to pay him with. The ranch was on its way out, even though we didn't know it at the time. The Jim Talbots were the first to go.

It hadn't always been that way. At first the land had been filled with life. Dad said that when they first moved out on the Washita the grass brushed the bottom of his stirrups as he rode. He and his brothers used to ride fenders and shoot prairie chickens and race greyhounds after coyotes, and in the winter the tanks were covered with ducks. We killed hogs in the chill of late fall mornings, and great flocks of blackbirds fanned and circled by the lot gate where we threw out feed for the cattle. But by 1932 the grass was short and spare, and the hot ground showed bare and caked, and the tanks were bogs of mud, or cracked dry. It was a land of horned toads and tumble bugs and killdeers, and the hot wind harried its surface without mercy. It would not support much life. It could not support the Jim Talbots.

A lot of dusted-out farmers went to the valleys of California during those bad years. Jim Talbot decided to stick with Texas. He moved south to work for another cousin, and to live in another two-room shack, on a farm near Taylor.

It didn't take long to load the family. Two rooms hold-

The Jim Talbots—Pearl, Jim and Frances

173

ing five people do not have much space left for extra furniture. They had a small four-hole wood stove with a stove-pipe oven, five chairs in all, a table, kitchen safe, and two beds, and that was about it. Jim had a few tools but he had always sharecropped or worked somebody else's place so he had no plows or harness.

It must have been a grim afternoon when Dad helped them load all their worldly possessions in the back of an old Chevy bob-tailed truck. But for Frances and me it was a time of excitement and expectation—a time of people talking and moving—and we were filled with thoughts of traveling and seeing new places and rolling merrily down the highway in another adventure together. While the grownups loaded the truck, we played Annie Over with a black sock stuffed with rags. We thought our world would always be the same.

They finished loading a little before sundown, that time of the day when the prairie took on a gentler countenance. The last things loaded were the two mattresses. The men laid them on top of all the furniture and made the back of the truck look like a big soft bed. Frances and I crawled up on top and played and rolled around till Dad hollered up at us to calm down. When we left the shack Pearl got in the cab and held the boy in her lap. He was squalling because he wanted in the back with us. The girl climbed up on the mattresses in the back of the truck. She sat in a corner by herself, kind of drawn up in a knot. I think she was crying.

We drove back to the ranch house at dusk, leaving the shack sitting empty and forsaken in the middle of the prairie space. Tumbleweeds were already slipping under the fence and huddling against its weathered walls.

Nobody talked much in our family anyhow, and there was even less talk that night at supper, even though Frances and I poked and giggled though the meal, and Frances knocked over her milk. After supper we played with Frances's doll on the back porch while Jim and Dad and Grandad sat on the steps and talked.

They spoke in low tones with long pauses between sentences. A coyote gave a few yaps somewhere out on the prairie and the windmill creaked and rattled. Otherwise for them it was a place of silence.

At bedtime Frances and I slept on a pallet in the front hall. We talked about the fun we were going to have on the trip and that maybe we would eat at a cafe. A mockingbird sang late into the night from the windmill top.

The next morning Dad put bows on the truck bed and tied a big wagon sheet over them, and the truck looked all the world like a covered wagon. It was cool and dark under the tarp, and even before it was tied down, Frances and her doll and I had circled up to play in the back corner. I had a boy doll with overalls but I never got it out when Frances was there. While we were playing, Jim's wife pushed in a cardboard box that had their traveling clothes in it. It was tied with binder twine.

Dad pulled the truck up by the windmill to top off the radiator and sent Frances and me after some drinking water. We got a couple of jugs to fill from the tank in the milk house. They were big, gallon vinegar jugs with towsacking wrapped around and sewed on for cover. As long as the towsacking was wet, the water stayed cool, and the jug had a good musty wet smell when you raised it to drink.

Grandmother and Pearl came out of the house. Pearl was carrying a shoe box of fried chicken and biscuits. Frances and I had filled the jugs and had crawled up the windmill ladder and were walking the crossbraces. Jim and Grandad stopped talking and shook hands. Pearl and Grandmother hugged each other, and as she turned to leave, Grandmother reached into her apron pocket and handed her a tin of snuff. Pearl got up in the cab and Jim told Frances to get down from the windmill and get in the truck. The other girl and the boy were sitting back in the corner under the wagon sheet when Frances and I crawled in and started wrestling around on the soft mattresses. We were anxious to begin this new game together.

We were doing somersaults when Dad told me to get down out of the truck. I climbed down and waited for him to send me after something for the trip, when he hugged me against his leg and told me to help Grandmother with the milking while he was gone. Then he crawled up into the cab and Jim pegged around to crank the truck. He jerked around till the engine coughed and popped and finally started running. Then he got up in the cab and they pulled out of the yard and rolled down the hill to the pasture road that led out to another world.

I stood and watched part of my life driving away and I couldn't move. I could not believe it. I couldn't believe that they—Dad and Jim Talbot and Frances—could drive off on this great adventure and leave me behind. I couldn't believe that Frances would go away and leave me in this lonesome place without anyone to play with.

Then a kind of panic struck me, and I ran after the truck as it bumped and swayed on the road that skirted the cow-lot fence. It slowed to cross the cattleguard that led to the next pasture and I almost caught up with it. But then the old truck started making dust and I stopped. I could see Frances sitting with her legs hanging over the back edge of the truck and the mattresses. She held up her hand for a wave and the tears rolled down her cheeks. I leaned against a fence post—aching and empty—and cried as I watched the old truck with its wanderers drive away through the prairie-dog town that was the top of the farthest hill I could see.

I never saw the Jim Talbots again. The dry prairie wind that blew the water out of the chicken troughs and sucked the moisture from the soil and the grass and any green thing that grew—crop or weed—blew away Frances and the Jim Talbots and that part of my life that they occupied.

The land got drier after that. The sand drifted deep against the fence rows, and the tumbleweeds rolled back and forth across the scorched prairie. The everlasting winds shifted around the compass, never bringing rain, always dust. The grasshoppers came and the government passed out 'hopper bait, but they still rose in waves as you walked along the stripped and tattered rows of cotton. The elm trees in the yard and all the fruit trees died, and we chopped them into firewood. The only tree left on the place was one lone cottonwood. Finally the windmill could no longer bring up water and the sucker rods rattled dryly in the pipes. The land died, and we moved away and left it lying there on the prairie.

The Depression ended, and it did finally rain again on the Washita but the hard times and the hot winds had dusted us out by then, and we weren't there to see it. I know it rained because I went back about thirty-five years later and looked at the old place, and I saw the grass.

I finally found the house place. I wound around through pastures and tied gates and cattleguards and came on it kind of unexpectedly. But there it was, or what was left, still sitting on the wind-swept hill, some frame barns and out buildings, looking down to the Washita River, a mile away. A cow lot was left, the red grain barn still had a fence around it. A long building that had two seed barns, a garage and a blacksmith shop, all joined, was still there. The cottonwood, not much bigger, was still there, but the house was gone, wrecked and hauled off. All that was left were three concrete steps leading up to nowhere and my grandmother's old Great Majestic iron stove sitting in what was once a daily-swept yard.

Alfonso's Yearly Routine

T. Lindsay Baker

Eagle-News
July 27, 1989

I found Alfonso Valadez from his sign.

Painted red and green on a white piece of plywood, the sign shows a stylized slice of watermelon and bears the beckoning words, "melons ahead." It leans against a utility pole on the east side of U. S. Highway 385 about two miles north of the Needmore cotton gin in Terry County on the Texas high plains.

Alfonso is in his late twenties. Standing almost six feet tall, he was bareheaded and wearing jeans and a blue plaid shirt when we met last weekend. The little toe from his right foot was showing through a worn place on the side of his blue canvas shoes. He's been coming to the Texas South Plains for the last six years to hoe cotton.

"Watermelons are a little on the side for cash," Alfonso explained to me. "We brought 'em from South Texas, from Rio Grande City. Friends grow 'em down there."

The fruit stand where I visited with Alfonso stood in a corn patch a little in front of a modest grey stucco house behind which was a corrugated sheet iron implement shed and three elm trees. The "stand" itself consisted of little more than a wooden sun shade with open sides on four spindly legs. Beneath it were three tables groaning under their heaps of melons.

Each summer Alfonso leaves home in the Rio Grande Valley to travel to the Texas high plains to hoe cotton. It is part of his yearly routine. Usually he comes with relatives.

"I come to work with my brother-in-law and his family," he said. "We're hoeing cotton, cleaning the cotton fields." Unless they are hoed, the fields can become clogged with weeds, strangling the growing cotton plants. No machine can remove the weeds so well as a trained worker with a hoe.

Alfonso spends his summers away from home hoeing cotton and peddling melons. "We migrate up here," he said, adding, "we'll go back down there August 30th, I think."

When he returns home to Rio Grande City, Alfonso will spend the autumn packing local produce in wooden crates for shipment around the United States. "I work in a packing shed . . . lettuce and tomatoes. I work about three months in September, October, November and December," he explained.

A roadside stand of watermelons near Seminole, Texas

When I asked what he did with his time the rest of the year, he replied, "I go fishing. That's all."

Each year Alfonso looks forward to leaving home for his three months on the high plains. "I like the weather. South Texas is much hotter than West Texas," he reported. Alfonso also likes the people in Terry County: "They're nice people up here. They treat you well. They're not prejudiced."

As he sat on the base of an old school desk beside his tables laden with melons, kicking the reddish brown dirt with his right foot, I asked Alfonso what he does for fun when he is so far away from home. His only reply was, "Sometimes we go to Lubbock . . . to the movies. That's all."

I gave Alfonso a five-dollar bill for one of his largest melons and headed south on U. S. 385. As I drove, I thought to myself about his yearly routine of hoeing cotton and packing produce half the year and then fishing and lounging around the rest of the time.

I think Alfonso might have the right idea.

Making the Rattlesnake Roundup Circuit

T. Lindsay Baker

Eagle-News
March 4, 1988

February starts the season . . . not for basketball or for football training camp, but for rattlesnake roundups in Texas.

Just the other day I had the chance to visit with Mrs. Pauline Howard of Midlothian, Texas, a regular at the rattlesnake roundups. "They run from mid-February to the first of May," she told me. "Cleburne is the first one," and it was at this event that we visited.

The reason for the snake appeal escapes me, but organized rattlesnake roundups have become part of the spring calendar throughout Texas.

The roundups began as rural affairs where service clubs offered prizes to the locals who came in with the largest or the most rattlesnakes. The events were scheduled in the spring, when the snakes began coming out of winter hibernation. Hunters brought them to the towns in big gunny sacks that looked alive with the squirming of the snakes inside.

Now there's a complete circuit of rattlesnake events, called "rattlesnake shows" by the insiders. Among the Texas towns that now feature them are Brownwood, Weatherford, Walnut Springs,

Lometa, Taylor, Cleburne, Breckenridge, San Angelo, Granbury, Freer, Laredo, San Saba, Gainesville, Midlothian, and Jacksboro.

Not all the participants are hunters. Others come along in vans and pickups with campers crammed with folding tables and all manner of rattlesnake merchandise.

Mrs. Howard at her booth was selling rattlesnake skin hat bands, belts, buckles, coin purses, handbags, cigarette cases, snuff can holders, eyeglass cases, paperweights, key rings, and rattlesnake rattle earrings. Her most unusual item was a transparent plastic toilet seat encasing baby rattlesnakes.

For the venturesome, the food concessions offered freshly killed deep-fried rattler meat.

Some of the other people come to rattlesnake shows because they simply enjoy snakes. As I visited with Mrs. Howard, she gestured toward an attractive dark-haired lady wearing a blue plaid blouse and holding a blanketed infant. "That lady there standing with the baby, her husband is the snake handler. He does the kiss of death with the cobra," she said.

Brett Crabb of Granbury, Texas, came over to join our conversation. He is best known in the rattlesnake circles for "doing the sleeping bag."

He explained to me that every outdoorsman has a fear of waking up in the middle of the night with a rattler that's come in from the cold to share a sleeping bag. Well, Brett does this in a big way.

As a rattlesnake show event, he crawls into an empty sleeping bag on the floor, after which other handlers stuff it full of live rattlesnakes as bedfellows.

"How many have you had in there?" I had to ask. He turned around to ask a friend what the largest number had been, and then said, "It was 223, plus four non-poisonous ones."

Next I asked what it was like.

"It was cool inside. The snakes are cold-blooded. It's like an air conditioner," he explained. "Everyone else was hot and sweating, but I felt real good."

Rayon Dresses and FDR

T. Lindsay Baker

The Clarendon News
August 9, 1990

Rayon dresses and Franklin D. Roosevelt don't normally seem like things that would go together in someone's mind, but they do in the remembrances of Jo Stewart Randel of Panhandle, Texas.

Jo's memories of the two things go back to a hot, muggy day in Amarillo, Texas, in July 1938. On that day, July 11 to be specific, President Franklin Roosevelt came to town.

Traveling through the plains country, ostensibly to observe Dust Bowl conditions, the president actually was going from place to place to lend support to Democratic primary candidates who supported his New Deal political programs.

Everyone in the Panhandle region seemed to have come to Amarillo to see the president. "It was in the Depression, and we'd been in the Dust Bowl," Jo related. "I don't know how to express the excitement we felt just to have him there," she said.

After the president's private railway car came to a halt at the Fort Worth and Denver depot, he was helped to a big Cadillac convertible for a parade down Polk Street through the heart of the city. A marching band 2,500 strong accompanied him. Among the crowd of 200,000 people was Jo Randel.

"I went with Mary Stocking and Bill McConnell," she said. "He was the district attorney then, and we were there with Curtis and Nadine Douglas." Douglas was an attorney with a second-story office overlooking Polk Street. "We got a good view from that lawyer's office about where the Paramount Theater is."

Following the parade, Jo and her friends drifted with the crowd to Uloid Park, where President Roosevelt was scheduled to speak. All the gentlemen were wearing their best suits, while the ladies wore the latest summer fashions—sheer rayon dresses.

"We all had on sheer black dresses. Mine was dotted with white, and some had other white trim. It had a full skirt, big puffed sleeves, and I wore a black straw hat," she remembered. "It was a sheer fabric that looked like chiffon. They were beautiful."

No sooner did the president arrive at Uloid Park than a shower began. The crowd loved seeing that Roosevelt, like them, simply stood there unshielded and let the warm rain come down. Standing in what became heavier rain were Fort Worth newspaper editor Amon G. Carter, Senator Tom Connally of Texas, and Texas Governor James V. Allred, whom Roosevelt had just appointed a federal judge. "After we got there it poured rain, but we wouldn't leave," Jo stated.

Rayon was a new fabric on the market in summer 1938, and the sheer dresses made from the fabric were among the first their wearers had owned. Most of them were unaware of its distinctive characteristic of shrinking upon becoming moistened.

As the audience stood in the rain, all looking toward the president, to the surprise and bemusement of everyone, the ladies' new rayon dresses started shrinking. Jo Randel tells the story best:

"The chiffon of our dresses pulled up to our hips. My dress must have been only five inches long. Beneath were our black slips. They all drew up. They all had them on."

The shrinking of her dress remains the most prominent memory of Jo Randel for the day FDR came to town. "I don't remember hearing him (the president) speak. The thing that really stuck in my mind was that my dress drew up."

A Collection of Poems

Jean Schnitz

Kingsville-Bishop Record News
October 5, 1971

The Day Before Christmas

'Twas the day before Christmas,
And all through the house
Every creature was stirring,
Even a mouse.
The children, wide-eyed, were all over the place
Laughing and fighting and running a race.
The sun shining outside on the grass did not beckon.
They wanted to guard all the presents, I reckon.
So they stayed in the house all over the rug,
'Till I sent them outside with a hug and a tug.
Santa must surely get on with the job
Of getting things ready for all of this mob.
He's fighting a long all-day uphill battle,
How can he have secrets when kids like to tattle?
Poor Santa at our house has trouble of sorts,
Getting in place all these millions of parts.
Heard his reindeer will be barked at by dogs,

They've never seen clothes that look like his togs!
But later tonite
With the kids out of sight
Ol' Santa will sigh,
And beg us goodbye,
And say, "Man, I sure do not jest!"
"Merry Christmas, it's your turn to rest!"

—December 24, 1970

Maybe Next Year

It's time for New Year's Resolutions,
For last year's problems we seek solutions,
The time we say what we will NOT do,
Or what we WILL do all the New Year through.
We try to start out the New Year right,
By declaring resolves on New Year's night.
Some folks may formally make a list,
Others just SAY what they'll try to resist.
Often the easiest thing to do,
Is to limit resolves to one or two,
And so this year I made only one,
Trying to keep it was not any fun.
I hope that you do better than I,
I hope that you are a much better guy,
Who won't so fast to temptation bow,
Please wait somewhat longer to break your vow.
I vowed that I would not write a rhyme,
But I cannot resist just one more time!

—January 3, 1971

The TV Tube Syndrome

One Sunday night as I looked all around,
A weird epidemic appeared to abound.
Each person I saw, especially guys,
Had something peculiarly wrong with their eyes.
I looked once again, and tried not to stare,
But I was not wrong, it really was there!
Eyeballs rectangular looked rather strange.
Whatever could happen to cause such a change?
It's really not hard to find out the reason,
It has to do with the long football season.
The changes began the day after New Year's
Football game watching does things to eye gears.
The TV Tube Syndrome has taken its tolls,
It happens each year after the Super Bowl!

—January 17, 1971

Such Weather!

This crazy weather,
Makes me so mad!
One day it's nice,
Next day it's bad.
We have a week of spring-like weather
Then back comes winter, cold as ever!

The wind just blows,
All day and night.
That's how it goes,
A losing fight.

The South wind blows the dirt away,
The North wind blows it back next day.

West Texas sand
Caliche, clay,
Black dirt, red dirt,
The sky looks gray.
Old Mexico lets us have its share,
This dirt will settle down somewhere.

South Texas is
A changing spot.
It gets too cold,
It gets too hot,
It gets too dry, we cry for rain,
It rains too much, we cry in pain!

The rain will come,
I'll bet my hat,
I won't say when,
I won't know that,
I've lived here much too long to say,
But it will surely rain someday.

—March 18, 1971

Garage Sales

The signs say, "Garage Sale,"
Now what do they mean?
More garages for sale
Than have ever been seen?
I'm the curious sort,

I decided to try.
So I went to some sales,
Not intending to buy.
I just wanted to see
Why such crowds gather round,
And you can be sure that
The reason I found.
I've never seen bargains
That even compare—
Hooray for garage sales,
Any time, anywhere!
The reason that some find
Garage sales a pleasure
Is that "One man's junk is
Another man's treasure!

—June, 1971

Yesterday, Today, and Tomorrow

Tomorrow never comes,
Or so the saying goes.
If truth this should become,
What problems it would pose!
With never any future,
There would never be a past,
Life would become a treadmill,
We'd be going nowhere fast.
If today is so important
That we never pass it by,
Neither finding dreams to reach for,
Nor feeling need to try,
We soon would feel quite beaten,

Life would be a hopeless bore.
Today, now and forever,
Just today, and nothing more.

We need to have our yesterdays
To cherish things we've done.
To profit by mistakes we've made,
To remember all the fun.
We need to have tomorrows
If our lives would have a plan,
With dreams, hopes, and ambitions
To achieve all that we can.
We need to have today, also,
But today goes by so fast!
We must not waste a minute
For today just will not last!
Let's work and plan and do our best
To have a better day,
For today is the tomorrow
That we spoke of yesterday.

—June 28, 1971

How to Write a Poem

A friend asked me, "How do you write a poem?"
How would I know?
Not wanting to seem dumb, I tried to show 'im,
Although it's so.
Take pencil and paper and think of a rhyme,
Away you go!
Put two lines together and try one more time!
Don't be so slow.

192

Iambic pentameter sounds rather nice,
Trochaic, also.
Dactylic tetrameter used once or twice,
Is good for show.
Think of a subject somewhere on the way,
Something you know.
It helps if the poem has something to say.
Knowledge bestow.

Decide on a form and then try out a code,
Dimeter, trimeter, sonnet, or ode,
Limerick or lyric, sublime and serene,
Or some other form that has never been seen.

A poem is something that's easy to write.
Behold and lo!
But most of them ought to be kept out of sight.
Wastebasket throw.

—July 29, 1971

Formula for Success

No race is run,
No game is won,
Till it's begun,
And then well done.

If you would win,
You've got to try.
The man who won't
Will not get by.

The man who can't
Cannot be dared,
Can't even try—
Perhaps he's scared.

The man who would
Would do his best.
He might not win,
But he would quest.

The man who could,
Could work and try.
He could not quit,
Nor sit and sigh.

The man who should,
But still will not,
Is least of all,
Is good for what?

The man who will,
Will meet the test.
Each day that comes
He'll do his best.

He may not win
All of the time,
But every day
He'll upward climb.

Gold Diggers

Patrick Dearen

The Midland Reporter-Telegram
July 18–19, 1982

CRANE—Crawl the squeeze ways of the shallow caves of Castle Gap and the moaning wind and creaking strata whisper centuries-old tales of bloodshed, lost fortunes and a thousand lives consumed by obsessive quests for its enigmas.

Here in western Upton County, where the mesas and rimrock of the Castle Mountains yawn open to the greasewood lowlands of the Pecos River and its famed Horsehead Crossing, men have spent decades searching for this mile-long pass's haunting secret. For some, it has served to keep them alive past their allotted "three score and ten." For others, it has led to trauma and death.

"There's people around here that's looked a lifetime for it," said Smokey Swift, who, from the time he began ranching within a mile of the gap as a twenty-five-year-old in 1934, has seen men ruled by the anticipation that "tomorrow" would be the day a legendary bonanza would run through their fingers. "Some people are convinced that treasure is out there—they're just *convinced*."

Even for prehistoric nomadic Indians, Castle Gap may have held mystique, this gaping slash between bluffs strewn with boulders like bodies on a battlefield. White men probably never pe rused the twin layers of strata rimming 3,141-foot Castle and King mountains until Spanish explorers dispatched by Captain Rabage y Teran ventured through in 1760. By 1800, hostile Comanches on the trail to Mexico figuratively smeared the walls with war paint.

Within half a century more, Castle Gap had become what Crane folklorist Paul Patterson, who was born in 1909, has dubbed "the Interstate 20 for a hundred years." Gold had been discovered in California, and a multitude of forty-niners stormed through en route to Horsehead Crossing twelve miles away. This rush of horse and human flesh resulted in one of the gap's many claims to lost treasure, according to Billy Rankin of Rankin, who first rode through on horseback as an eighteen-year-old in 1926.

"I talked to one man who went through Castle Gap in the 1849 gold rush," he recalled, sitting in a quaint cafe in Rankin as his eyes squinted in recollection. "He was too young to remember when his parents took him out, but he remembered when he

Castle Gap. Photo by Patrick Dearen

came back through. They were supposed to have had horseshoe kegs full of gold, and one of them got lost. He came back in 1929 or 1930—he was an old man then—looking for that place where the horses may have watered, thinking they may have kicked it overboard."

The old man searched, those eighty years later, but the rocky battlements that gave Castle Gap its name held fast this secret.

Butterfield Overland Mail coaches carved their ruts in the gap from 1858–1861 on twenty-five-day blitzes from Tipton, Missouri, to San Francisco. By 1866 it was not uncommon to find bleached bones baking in the Castle Gap sun, as real-life Gil Favors drove thousands of cattle to northern markets along the Goodnight-Loving Trail.

But 1867 proved the most pivotal of all years in the tales of Castle Gap which men spin around campfires, where truth may be as fleeting as the lapping flames or as pungent as the liquor that tempers their speech.

That was the year the spirits of Castle Gap brought together two vastly different factions—Mexican emperor Maximilian's entourage fleeing Mexico with great wealth, and six vanquished Confederate solders escaping carpetbagger rule in Missouri.

According to early Sterling County settler T. J. Kellis (as recorded in J. Frank Dobie's *Coronado's Children*), the two parties met at Presidio del Norte on the Rio Grande in the Big Bend. The fifteen wagoners had pushed their animals hard, but it was only in prelude to a more desperate struggle to follow.

Seeking safe passage through Indian country and on to Galveston and a waiting ship, Maximilian's subordinates enlisted the Missourians as guards for what they termed a "valuable cargo of flour." Soon, the rugged, lawless land of the Trans-Pecos swallowed the groups.

Ruled by cynicism and bitterness, the ex-Rebels soon became suspicious, for the Austrians and Mexicans were careful never to leave the covered cargo unattended. Investigating secretly, the Missourians learned the truth—at their fingertips lay a fabulous fortune in gold and silver bullion, vessels, and Austrian, Mexican, and American coins.

Beyond Horsehead Crossing, Castle Gap was the lone break in a range of parched mountains, and on a pitch-black night the Missourians splattered the pass with blood, massacring the Maximilian party and burning the bodies in a fire of wagons and crates.

Now possessing an immense fortune as well as knowledge of its origin through papers found in a chest, the murderers faced a dilemma. The cargo had value not in these ravine-slashed hills of greasewood and catclaw, but only in civilization, where to display such wealth would lead to hangman's nooses.

Taking only what they could easily conceal, the men buried the rest, carefully sketching in their minds the rocks, sands and a lake bed. Mounting up, they rode into the rising sun, with plans to return once they decided how to dispose of such riches discreetly.

But the guarding spirits of Castle Gap must have frowned on their horrid deed, for during the rigorous journey, one man became so violently ill that he took refuge at Fort Concho, site of modern-day San Angelo. When his illness subsided, he rode after his companions and made a grisly discovery—their rotting bodies, mutilated by Indians, a day's ride out of Fort Concho.

Now the sole possessor of Maximilian's treasure, as well as of haunting memories, the man wandered northeast, hoping to make his way to Missouri and enlist the aid of Frank and Jesse James in claiming the bonanza. Near Denton he too fell victim to the spirits, as he camped by chance with three or four men who were horse thieves. Captured by a posse, he was thrown in jail, where his malady overcame him again.

On the verge of death, the man was examined by a Dr. Black, who gave him no chance for recovery as long as he remained behind bars. A lawyer named O'Connor was summoned to arrange his release, but before the attorney could undertake legal action, the Missourian's condition worsened. Baring conscience and soul, he told the two men of the Castle Gap massacre, sketched a map of the treasure's location—and died.

Astounded, Black and O'Connor undertook an expedition to Castle Gap, but by the time they arrived, violent sandstorms had so ravaged the land that the map was useless. All the men found were wagon irons—charred by fire.

And the legend had begun.

This basic tale of bloodshed and mystery is repeated often, with many variations. The August–September 1964 edition of *Frontier Times* indicated that the sole ex-Rebel survivor was named Bill Murdock. The Quest—An Exploration Corporation, of Tarzana, California, reported that his name was Hart and that he died in San Angelo, not Denton, of a gunshot wound after his arrest for horse theft. Although agreeing that the deathbed map went to a doctor and a lawyer, Quest contended that their names were Bradford Walters and Henry Jamison, respectively.

In the version long in circulation in the Castle Gap area, the five Missourians were killed not by Indians, but by Texas Rangers after a chase that took them all the way to Fort McKavett on the San Saba River. There was a survivor, all right—"You know, they always leave one to tell the tale," said Paul Patterson—but to confuse matters more, the man named Black was not a doctor but a ranger, said Billy Rankin.

And so the stories go, fact and fiction interwoven so closely that they are as indistinguishable as the point at which a campfire's yellow flames supercede those of blue.

But like those flames, legends can burn themselves indelibly into the minds of men.

"There was a fellow came in there at Castle Gap about 1929," recalled Rankin. "I lived over west out in the flats, seven, eight, ten miles away. He and these other people supposedly had a map about where the treasure supposedly was buried. This fellow at my place was supposed to be *a son of one of the outlaws that had killed Maximilian's troops*. But I don't know."

In the ensuing months, the man searched the deeply scored canyon for the secret that had died with his father.

"It was supposed to have been buried at the south side of the gap at a spring," said Rankin. "But there wasn't a spring there when I was first through there in 1926. But they'd had a stage stand there and were supposed to have gotten water from a spring.

"He looked and looked, but if he ever found any more than pig tracks, I don't know what it was. Some people thought for a long time that a wagon train burned there, but this old fellow said it was a corn train. I never did see any ruins of that wagon train."

Smokey Swift told of a Crane man who discovered a woman said to be an *eyewitness* to the massacre.

"Back in 1929 Swede Anderson brought an old Mexican woman, eighty, ninety years old, out from El Paso," he remembered. "Paid her expenses and everything. She was supposed to be a survivor of that ambush. When she got here she looked things over and told him, 'It's on that round mountain around the point between Crane and McCamey,' but to leave it alone, that the spirits would get 'em if they bothered it."

But even the spirits flee before the onrush of gold seekers, and extensive digs into the mountain's bedrock failed to turn up the cache. Or had the spirits simply led them astray?

A year or two later, remembered Swift, two men from Illinois came to the gap. Presumably, they had first-hand knowledge of the last surviving Missourian—for they were said to be *the actual pair who had received his deathbed map*. One was named Whitey; time dimmed Swift's memory concerning the second man's identity.

"They spent three years digging for that stuff out here," said

Swift. "They had twenty- to thirty-foot-deep holes. One of 'em died here; the other one finally left."

And empty-handed, but for calluses.

Whitey and his partner were among the earliest to conduct extensive searches for Maximilian's fortune, but they only foreshadowed the deluge to come. "I'll bet you there's a thousand or two over the last forty years looking," said Swift. "They dig more on my place (adjacent to the pass) than they do at the gap itself. Most of the digging takes place within a mile or two of the gap. We've had all types, every type in the world, digging out there. There's not a month of the year goes by without somebody coming down here digging."

Although Swift discovered homemade wagon wheel irons one-half mile south of the stage stand ruins in 1935, he never became caught up in the gold fever that can rule a man's life. But he can reel off story after story of those who did.

"I had one old man spend the whole winter out here in about 1937, digging between Castle Gap and Horsehead Crossing," he recalled. "He was convinced it was buried before they ever got to the gap."

Maybe so, but the greasewood plains failed to yield anything but sand.

On another occasion, Swift approached the stage ruins on horseback and came across "an ol' boy who'd just found a Mexican coin about the size of a dime, dated 1850-something." Then on a blazing summer day in 1974, a television technician and his wife, fresh from "digging on the halves" at Swift's ranch, banged on his door.

"'Mr. Swift,' they told me, 'we're fixin' to hit that treasure,'" he recalled. "I went out with 'em and they found a cap and ball pistol in a holster, ten or twelve feet underground."

Even while tempting with a coin here, a pistol there, the spirits continued to shield Castle Gap's true secrets. Still, they must have winced at the ravages of technology, which has almost gutted Castle Mountain and the gorge below. The most ambitious dig came in 1968, when two Amarillo brothers probed then-Castle Gap Park, a 100-acre tract leased to Upton County by the Caton Jacobs family. Assuring county officials they would dig but one "small hole at one location," the brothers used a backhoe to carve a modest, twenty-square-foot opening in the ravine below the historical marker.

Then gold fever seized the men, and with a bulldozer they slashed another canyon through Castle Gap, one forty feet deep, eighty feet wide and sixty yards long.

And Maximilian's treasure still remained unturned.

The spirits must have laughed.

Today, unfilled, the massive excavation bears mute testimony to the extent to which man will go in search of a legend.

But as in many legends, the spirits never smile on those who seek, only on those they choose. Such is the case of a cowboy whom Rankin first heard about decades ago:

"On the TX Ranch there was a Mexican boy, a horse wrangler, and his horses got out from ranch headquarters eight or ten miles away from Castle Gap and he went looking for them," he narrated. "This wrangler supposedly found a gold brick four or five miles northwest of the gap, in a cave at the point, toward Crane (from McCamey)."

Not realizing it was gold, continued Rankin, the wrangler retained it as a keepsake, and when he settled in Uvalde many years later, he used it as a doorstop. Making a grocery delivery to his home one day, a young man recognized the brick for what it was and purchased it at a nominal price from the Mexican, now elderly.

With the money from the gold bar, said Rankin, the delivery boy supposedly "got his first start"—which led him all the way to the vice presidency of the United States.

His name? John Nance Garner.

Other unsubstantiated reports of finds have filtered down through the years, including that of one lucky Upton County man, according to Paul Patterson.

"They say a man from McCamey—it's always 'they say'—dug up a few gold coins, eight or ten, in a can," he recalled. "Now as to whether or not it was part of Maximilian's treasure, nobody knows. Some thought it might have been connected with a train robbery. I personally never saw anybody show anything they found."

Whenever folks in the Pecos River country speak of Castle Gap, one name always dominates—Cliff Newland, who, with witching rod and a skilled eye, searched the bluffs and eroded canyon for decades.

"He spent a lifetime digging for that out there," said Swift. "It kept him alive until he was almost ninety-four. I had to take him out there once a week when he got feeble. He always had markers to go by. He'd say, 'You see that arrow out there on that mountain?' And he'd point it out and I couldn't see a thing."

Despite the notoriety of Maximilian's treasure, it was another lode that lured Newland.

"Cliff said that Maximilian's gold had been dug up," related Patterson, whose book *Pecos Tales* quotes Newland on the matter. The Maximilian bonanza, said Newland, was uncovered by "two fellers from Santone with four-horse wagon and two or three saddle horses. Stayed for eight weeks. Went back and bought ranches. Went around dressed up from then on."

The object of Newland's quest was the Catholic Cross Cache— gold bars, diamonds, and vases supposedly buried in 1780 by priests fleeing Mexico. A firm believer in symbols, signs, and stone scratchings, Newland found fuel for his search when laborers unearthed an inscribed rock near Big Spring. "Look for huge cross, 77," it said, "then look for V-shaped mountain."

Aware of a legend which said that etchings on a grave stone pointed to a grotto holding the Catholic Cross hoard, Newland centered his search on Castle and King mountains' cratered rimrock.

"One time Cliff Newland found a cave closed in by rocks, and just knew he'd found it," remembered Swift.

But he hadn't—nor did he ever.

"You know, ol' Cliff was always just one step away from it—the next day was always gonna be it," recalled Patterson. "That kept him going forty years."

But if a report in the November 11, 1927, *San Angelo Daily Standard* is true, Newland's lifelong search may have been in vain from the start. "A youth who is said to have a map of the exact location of the cache," said the article, "came here only to find that it had been removed, with indications that the removal had been made a short time previously."

Fact, fantasy, truth, fiction. Where does one end and another begin?

In the Pecos River country, sometimes the blend is as smooth as the colors in a summer sunset.

Though Castle Gap rocked with stampedes and gunfire more than a century ago, the pass is silent today except for the howl of the wind. Insofar as can be proven, it has yet to relinquish its riches, but that only serves to whet the appetites of seekers.

Are the treasures there? Do the answers lie buried under the rimrock? Or do the explanations lie in the liquor that leads men to embellish the truth around campfires?

The old-timers who have seen men come and go while Castle Gap's secrets abide are skeptical.

"Well, I kinda believe there must've been something there at one time," said Patterson. "But I'm kinda like Cliff—I think somebody must've got it. I don't believe there's anything now. With all this modern equipment, they surely must've found it."

"I'm satisfied that if wages had been paid for all the hours spent looking," opined Rankin, "it'd be a durn sight more than any treasure buried there. There's been more time lost hunting it than it was worth if they'd found it. I haven't kicked a rock over looking for it. Now, if I was riding a horse through and he kicked a rock over and there it was, well, I'd stop and reach down and get it—but I'm not going to help him kick any over."

"According to history, it's supposed to be there if somebody hasn't got it," said Swift. "I wouldn't say it's not there, but I wouldn't spend ten minutes looking for it. I've never turned a shovel looking for it and I'm not going to either."

But the believers still flock to Swift's ranch, still explore these hills of legend.

"It's something people want to believe—they're fanatics," he suggested, and then he lifted his eyes toward Castle Gap's guarding rimrock. "When I'm dead and gone, they'll still be hunting— I'm sure they will."

And Castle and King mountains will still look down on the gap, their riddles safely sealed and guarded by their spirits.

Chicken-fried Steak Tour Through Texas

Alan Solomon

Albuquerque Journal
Wednesday, November 4, 1998

BANDERA, Texas—It is the perfect food for those of us who figure we're all gonna die anyway, might as well die smiling and with a world-class gut.

It is red meat. It is dipped in cholesterol and coated with flour and fried in very hot oil. It is covered with thick, white, creamy gravy—gravy that can also be ladled over the mashed potatoes (traditional) or the french fries (perfect).

There's usually a vegetable. Green beans (from a can) are best, though corn (from a can) is acceptable, and okra—breaded and deep-fried (from a freezer)—is a special treat and, being fried, adds a nice nutritional touch. Thousand or French on the salad. Soft dinner rolls.

And tea. Iced—though you don't say "iced" when you order; in Texas, "iced" with tea is as redundant as "Texas" with longhorn. Free refills.

The entire experience is Chicken-fried Steak.

What is chicken-fried steak? It is steak fried like chicken is fried when it's fried right, which is why it's called what it is. It's been around for a while.

"I wish I could put a date on it," said Joyce Gibson Roach, author (with Ernestine Sewell Linck) of *Eats, a Folk History of Texas Foods* (Texas Christian University Press). One frontier soldier, she said, described Texans throwing meat into a vat of hot lard. "And he was just appalled at that sort of thing."

Breading it made it chicken-fried. Country-fried steak? Same thing, sometimes battered rather than breaded, and mostly in places like Alabama.

"I know it confuses a lot of Yankees and foreigners, because they think it's chicken," said Annetta White, who is responsible for the marvel that can be found at the Broken Spoke in Austin. "Now, some people have changed the name to 'country-fried,' but it's still Southern-fried chicken and it's still chicken-fried steak."

And it is still wonderful.

Sure, it can kill you if you eat it three times a day every day for eighty-seven consecutive years (and I say this fully aware of the legal fees generated by Cattlemen vs. Oprah), but it is nonetheless wonderful.

Earlier this year, while on another assignment in the Texas Hill Country, against the wishes of my wife and without first consulting a physician, I ate six chicken-fried steaks in five days.

The restaurants were chosen based on recommendations from pals in Houston, which is not in the Hill Country but is a good restaurant town once you stop sweating; and from Texas motel clerks, gas station attendants, cafe waitresses and, a couple of times, because the places looked good from the outside and I was hungry. There was nothing scientific about this survey. The best chicken-fried steak in Texas might be in Amarillo, for all I know.

But here's where I ate 'em and here's what I found:

• Andy's Diner, Fredericksburg. A couple of blocks off the kitsch-glutted main drag, this is a cafe, but a big one, that has been around for forty years and at lunchtime is packed with locals. The steak is "country-fried" on the menu, but that's because it was a "country café" in a previous life and the signature dish's name stuck. Don't fret; the chicken-fried, like Andy's, is the genuine article.

• Broken Spoke, Austin. It is a restaurant in front, a bar in the middle, a little museum on the side (lots of cool junk, including one of LBJ's hats and a chicken-fried steak plate autographed by singer Randy Travis) and a no-place-but Texas dance hall in back. There cannot be a better chicken-fried steak on the planet nor a better place to eat one.

• Hill Country Cupboard, Johnson City. Billboards say it has the "World's Best Chicken-Fried Steak." It also says "Over 36 served." The second part, though undoubtedly true, is meant as a joke; the first part got me in the door. Not great but pretty good, and the meat's tenderness would bring me back. The secret? Explained Monica, the waitress: "It's just beat real good."

• Lost Maples Cafe, Utopia. A little spot in a little Hill Country town too small to make any but the biggest road maps. At least ninety percent of the people who find Utopia took a wrong turn at Bandera; the rest probably came looking for the Lost Maples Cafe. The search is worth it. Said Linda, who served me my chicken-fried, on why only Texans make them this good: "Because nobody else knows how."

• O.S.T. Cafe, Bandera. The old bar doesn't have chairs or stools; it has saddles. If you drink (or eat) at the bar, you're staring into the nostrils of a dead elk. In short, the joint looks terrific and the back room is named for John Wayne. "I'd tell you where he sat," said the cashier, "but I'd be lying." Its chicken-fried steak is called The Duke. The Duke would not have been pleased. It's from a formed and frozen patty and chews like it. "We're really better known for our Mexican food," the cashier said.

• Threadgill's, Austin. Janis Joplin hung out at the original location, once a Gulf gas station. You can still see what it was, but it's been slicked up so much that the difference between the original on North Lamar and its much newer downtown location isn't all that much. And neither, despite a mound of clippings, was my chicken-fried steak. A chef familiar with the product called it "cafeteria food": "I believe in seasoning."

Your basic 'recipe'

Understand, there's no such thing as a truly bad chicken-fried steak, but there are essentials to doing it just right.

The steak must be intact beef steak, not chopped beef or soy-protein-laced hybrid, and fresh, never frozen. Round steak is the popular choice.

"Ours is hand-cut," said Don Wise, owner of Andy's, and a former butcher who cuts his own. "That makes a difference."

It must be pounded (sometimes with a vengeance) into submission, or carefully tenderized. This is old-time, humble home cooking—its creator, folklore to the contrary, is lost in history—and old-time, humble home cooking means making tough things edible.

Now we go to the Broken Spoke's Annetta White.

"We do what they call a double dip," she said. "Our flour is mixed with a cracker meal. This keeps the flour from matting too badly. Salt and pepper's all mixed in there.

"So you put your meat in there. Then you dip it in your egg and buttermilk—like six eggs to a gallon of buttermilk. Then you go back to your flour mixture."

Then it's ready to fry.

"A true chicken-fried steak would be fried in a skillet," Wise said.

"An iron skillet keeps the oil hot," agreed a manager of a Fredericksburg motel who obviously knew her stuff (and, to prove it, had sent me to Andy's).

But busy places like Andy's and the Broken Spoke, which may hand-bread hundreds of the things every mealtime, have to deep-fry. Only Momma would know the difference.

It must be served hot and right now. Crunch is essential. Also, the white cream gravy, when it cools, clots (which it undoubtedly does in your body as soon as it senses an artery, but you won't see that, so don't worry about it); hot steak helps keep the gravy molten.

The gravy is simple, but the steak wouldn't be real without it.

"Gravy and chicken-fried steak is like Bob Wills and western swing country music," said James M. White, who built the Spoke in 1964 and runs it with his wife, Annetta.

Wills, by the way, played the Broken Spoke three times in the late 1960s. George Strait got his start there, playing for $400 a night. It's that kind of place.

"We're the home of the best chicken-fried steak in town," White said. "We ain't got no Perrier water or hangin' fern baskets, but we got cold beer and good whiskey and good-lookin' girls to dance with."

Back to gravy.

"The main thing with Southern white gravy is, if I was doing it at home, I'd use my meat drippings," said Annetta White. "But at the Spoke, we use our grease that we fry our cutlets in."

She makes it twice a day, in three-gallon batches, which would require a lot of drippings.

"You put your flour and your salt and your pepper in there, and you kind of brown it, so that your flour cooks. Then we put in whole milk. We just cook that until it thickens."

A puddle of that thick gravy goes on the steak, a little more on the potatoes, maybe a little more on the side for dipping, and there it is. (And yes, everyone knows this isn't broccoli with a spritz of lemon juice.)

"You know what I tell people? 'It's OK. You can't eat 'em every day, but walk an extra mile,'" said Annetta White. "Everybody's got to enjoy food once in a while."

Heaven? That's chicken-fried steak.

With a big ol' Texas smile.

RECIPE

This recipe for Chicken Fried Steak was adapted from "Spirit of The West," by Beverly Cox and Martin Jacobs.

CHICKEN-FRIED STEAK

Preparation time: 35 minutes
Cooking time: 18 minutes
Yield: 4 servings

STEAKS:
1/2 cup all-purpose flour
1/2 teaspoon salt, or to taste
Freshly ground black pepper
1 large egg, beaten with 2 tablespoons water
3/4 cup buttermilk baking mix, such as Bisquick
4 pieces bottom or top round steak (about 2 pounds), pounded
    thin to tenderize
1/3 cup vegetable oil, plus more as needed

GRAVY:
2 tablespoons meat drippings, bacon drippings or lard
3 tablespoons all-purpose flour
1 can (12 ounces) evaporated milk
1/2 cup water

1/2 teaspoon salt, or more to taste
Freshly ground black pepper

Stir together flour, salt and pepper to taste in shallow pan or plate. Place egg mixture in another shallow pan. Place baking mix in third shallow pan. Coat steaks in flour mixture; dip in egg-water mixture. Coat with baking mix.

Heat oil in large, non-stick skillet over medium-high heat until a sprinkle of water sizzles. Add steaks, in batches, until golden brown and cooked through, 4 to 5 minutes per side, adding more oil if needed. Remove from pan; keep warm. Keep meat drippings in pan.

For gravy, heat drippings over medium heat. Add flour. Cook, stirring constantly, until flour turns golden, 2 to 3 minutes. Add milk and water. Cook, stirring constantly, until smooth and thickened, about 5 minutes. Season with salt and pepper. Serve gravy with steaks.

DATA PER SERVING: Calories 790, percent calories from fat 46, carbohydrates 40 g, fat 40 g, cholesterol 210 mg, protein 65 g, saturated fat 12 g, sodium 1,120 mg, fiber 1 g

Cowboy Poet
Honored by Peers

=========================== **Peggy McCracken**

Pecos Enterprise
March 4, 1998

Pecos—Paul Patterson nearly dropped his few remaining teeth when he heard his biography being read during the awards ceremony at the thirteenth annual Texas Cowboy Poetry Gathering in Alpine Saturday.

The eighty-eight-year-old (nearly eighty-nine) writer attended all three days of the gathering, reading some of his new poetry, plus some old favorites by request—a poem from *High Wide and Then Some*.

When the widow of a famous poet, the late Buck Ramsey, was called to the podium during the awards ceremony, Patterson thought Ramsey was to receive the Heritage Award posthumously.

But not so. When he heard Mrs. Ramsey begin the biography detailing his birthdate and place "and what I had done and hadn't done," Patterson realized he was the man of the hour.

"I'm the oldest one still alive, if I am alive, and they awarded me that," Patterson modestly opined.

Although he's written six books of poetry, two novels, a children's book and articles in numerous book compilations,

Patterson said his main claim to literary fame is noted Western writer Elmer Kelton, whom he taught in high school.

"I taught him more than I know myself about writing," Patterson said.

Elmer was just out of high school when Patterson published his first book, *Sam Magoo.*

"I sold it for just $2, but it died early of poor circulation," Patterson said of *Magoo.* "Now a freshman at Sul Ross State University said he paid $150 for a copy."

His second book, *Crazy Women in the Rafters*, is out of print, but the printer sells it for $100 per copy—none of which Patterson gets.

"I didn't even make my money back on that one," he said. "It didn't pay until the second printing, and it didn't have a second printing."

Old age has slowed Patterson to the point he attends only two cowboy poetry gatherings a year—Alpine and Lubbock. He no longer travels to Arizona and several gatherings in New Mexico. The rarefied air in Ruidoso is too much for him nowadays, he said.

He and his wife, Marjorie, live in Pecos full time now at 512 S. Oleander, except for an occasional visit to Crane to "pay my bills." They have a home provided for them in Crane, and "It is hard to look a gift house in the mouth," said the witty writer.

Patterson's Heritage Award leather notepad cover was hand tooled at the Big Bend Saddlery in Alpine. It sports an engraved silver orb with the inscription "Texas Cowboy Poetry Gathering, 1998."

With his name in block letters on the front, Patterson is not too worried about someone else mistaking it for his own.

Telling "Tales" Keeps Patterson Busy and Happy

=== **Rosie Flores**

Pecos Enterprise
March 18, 1997

P ECOS, TEXAS—He considers himself "just an ordinary writer," but his readers think otherwise.

Paul Patterson has been telling "tales" for most of the century. He was born March 28, 1909, in the drifting sands of Gaines County, just a few miles east of the New Mexico Territory.

J. D. Patterson, Paul's father, and his family drifted down into Reagan County, Upton County, Mitchell County, Nolan County, Reeves County, Pecos County and shortly, back to Upton county, not to mention the twenty-odd moves within this area.

"These moves being at a snail's pace in a covered wagon, one would assume that I spent half my life just riding around," said Patterson.

He earned a high school diploma, 1929, in Rankin and a B. A. degree from Sul Ross College.

A 1935 Sul Ross graduate, Patterson did graduate work in Geneva, Switzerland, and at the University of Texas, Utah State University, The National University of Mexico, The University of Madrid and The University of Buffalo, New York.

He attributes his yearning for learning to a big, gray A. C. Hoover horse who threw him into a hillside in 1931 and "knocked some sense" into him.

A teacher for over forty years, he claims his most famous student is, perhaps, Elmer Kelton, who has been known to say, "Paul taught me everything I know . . . and everything I write has a little bit of Paul Patterson in it."

"I don't know if I taught him all that much, but he says I did," said Patterson.

As past president of the Texas Folklore Society, Patterson encourages young people to study folklore and is known as one of the foremost folk humorists in the U. S. today. In perhaps the highest of accolades given to any person of Texas letters, Patterson has been proclaimed the poet "Lariat" of Texas.

Patterson states that he feels like "he's done it all." Everything from being a cowboy, cook, house painter, small-time radio scriptwriter, small-time rodeo announcer, tale teller at festivals and cowboy symposiums and forty-one months as coder-decoder of secret messages for the 12th Air Force and twenty-nine months in North Africa and Italy in World War II.

Patterson has written ten books, five of which publishers nationwide continue to declare, "no account." He has written five books of cowboy rhymes, one book for children and numerous articles and essays for periodicals.

At eighty-five, he is a proud half-citizen of two small West Texas towns, Crane and Pecos.

"I live half of the time in Crane and half in Pecos, when we're not traveling around," said Patterson.

He doesn't exactly fit the description of an old-time cowboy, but he has punched cows, herded sheep and ridden broncos with the best of them.

"I still remember those cowboy days along the Pecos River like they happened yesterday," he said.

Patterson never gained much fame as a cowboy, but he has gained some popularity as a writer, poet and folklorist.

His tales of the early days on horseback or around the chuck wagon, many told in rhyme, can keep a bunch of people laughing until they cry.

"My poems can run from being totally true to tolerably true to totally false," he said.

He has four volumes of cowboy poetry in the series *A Pecos River Pilgrim's Poems*, on the market, and Volume IV carries a mostly true tale about a West Texas cowboy named Gid Redding who had a special way with rattlesnakes, taming horses, cooking grub and handling little pigs so they wouldn't squeal.

"These are the ones I enjoy telling the most, because you never know if the tale is true or not, but it could go either way," he said laughing.

Patterson's story about Redding, who died a couple of years ago, is a great story about what makes this part of Texas so interesting.

As Patterson recalls, the newspaper story goes something like this: "A tall man with his face swathed in adhesive tape (or some such) and riding a black horse robbed the bank of Hatch, New Mexico, of $5,000.

"The man turned out to be Gid Redding, the man with whom I batched on the Hoover Horse Ranch out of Buena Vista part of the previous winter," said Patterson. "In any case, the following fall I drew my $22 in wages and enrolled in Sul Ross College, whereas Gid, harboring higher ambitions and hankering for bigger, faster money, rode in and robbed that bank. A cowboy compadre is said to have said to him: 'Gid, if I was going to rob a bank, I'd a took it all.' But Redding responded, 'I didn't owe but $5,000.'"

According to Patterson, Redding didn't smoke, cuss, drink and most especially didn't chase women.

"In fact, women were the only creatures on this earth he was boogered of. At least he never married that I know of," Patterson said. He attended his friend's funeral at Monahans, where he died at the age of ninety-one.

While cowboying together on the Hoover place, Patterson said Redding did the cooking while he took care of the outdoor work—feeding twenty-two saddle horses and rustling (herding) other horses. "It was an ideal cowboy spread. No cow to milk and no eggs to gather," he said.

Patterson tried to get Redding to let him write his memoirs, but the man wouldn't allow it. Although a lot of stories abound about Redding, he only talked about mundane things, Patterson said.

Redding is said to have taken flying lessons—for which he owed money—and to have flown from one side to the other during the Mexican Revolution. He was reportedly shot down during one of the flights and it took him eight days to walk out of Mexico. When he went back to Ozona to settle up his debts (some say after the bank robbery), people would ask him how he was getting along.

"Walkin' the golden streets," was his stock reply, Patterson said.

Redding was a noted bronco buster and horse trainer, and Patterson praises his long ago line camp companion with being one of the best.

"Train up a horse in the way Gid Redding sayeth and he will not depart from it," Patterson wrote in the preface of his latest poetry volume.

Patrick Dearen of Midland, a noted author in West Texas, has written the foreword for Patterson, who is publishing a three-volume set of books titled, *A Bouquet of Biscuits*.

In his foreword, Dearen writes, "His stories are dust devils that carry readers 'somewhere over the Pecos' to a West Texas Oz born of folklore and satire.

"To a wide spectrum of Southwesterners, he is known simply as 'Paul' or 'Mr. Pat,' this beloved tale-teller who has spent a lifetime living and exploring the humor and legends of the Pecos. Behind his byline, his anecdotal slices of life become the offbeat and the unforgettable."

Although Patterson has collected folklore from across the Southwest, he also has done his part in these volumes to ensure that new tales continue to spring forth, according to Dearen.

Patterson also enjoys doing book reviews, speaking to clubs and organizations and plain "reminiscing."

"My favorite is reciting poetry and telling tales at cowboy gatherings," said Patterson.

"I truly enjoy folklorico, you can interpret it the way you see it and it doesn't matter if it's a 'tall tale' or the truth," he said.

Contributors

F. E. Abernethy is a Regents Professor Emeritus at Stephen F. Austin State University and is Secretary-Editor of the Texas Folklore Society. He is author of *Singin' Texas; Texas Folklore Society, 1909–1943: Volume I; Texas Folklore Society, 1943–1971, Volume II,* and editor of numerous Texas Folklore Society Publications and *Tales of the Big Thicket.*

T. Lindsay Baker is the Director of the Texas Heritage Museum in Hillsboro. He is the author of several books, including *Ghost Towns of Texas* and *The Polish Texans.* His articles have appeared in newspapers ranging from the *Daily News* in Galveston to the *Globe-Times* in Amarillo. For several years he syndicated his feature entitled "T for Texas," which was published across the state.

Kent Biffle is one of the most widely-read journalists in the state. He is a long-time member of the Texas Folklore Society and has attended and written about the TFS annual meetings for many years. Often his columns are about individuals and subjects that he encounters and develops at the meetings. He ranges far and wide across the state, and sometimes into adjoining states, for *The Dallas Morning News.* His columns have been collected in *A Month of Sundays.*

James W. Byrd writes a weekly column in *The Commerce Journal* after many years of producing books and articles for academic publications. He is the author of *J. Mason Brewer: Negro Folklorist* and was responsible for bringing America's most important African-American folklorist back to his home state of Texas in the years before Brewer died in 1975.

Lawrence Clayton, a past president of the Society, has published on the subjects of the literature, life, and lore of the cowboy and ranch life in the West, with emphasis on Texas. His publications include *Historic Ranches of Texas, Cowboys, Benjamin Capps and the South Plains, Elmer*

Kelton, and *Longhorn Legacy*. In addition he has edited a number of volumes including *Horsing Around* and *The March to Monterrey*. He and his wife, Sonja Irwin Clayton, have begun issuing a series of pamphlets on ranch life in their area under the general rubric "Fort Griffin Sketches."

Mike Cox is a nationally published author, syndicated newspaper columnist, rare book dealer, public speaker and trainer. His books include *Historic Austin: An Illustrated History*; *Fred Gipson: Texas Storyteller*; and *The Confessions of Henry Lee Lucas*. He writes a monthly book review column, "Texana," which appears in four newspapers. He currently is Chief of Media Relations for the Texas Department of Public Safety.

Patrick Dearen grew up in Sterling City, Texas, and earned a journalism degree from The University of Texas. He worked for the *San Angelo Standard-Times* and the *Midland Reporter-Telegram* before becoming a freelance writer and publishing several books about West Texas history and folklore. He is the author of four novels, including *When Cowboys Die*, a finalist for the Spur Award of Western Writers of America. He lives in Midland with his wife Mary, assistant city editor of the *Midland Reporter-Telegram*.

Robert J. (Jack) Duncan is a freelance writer whose work has been published in *Reader's Digest, Chicken Soup for the Country Soul* and elsewhere. A believer in lifelong learning, he recently earned a second master's degree. He is a former president of the Texas Folklore Society. Jack is married to his McKinney (Texas) High School sweetheart, Elizabeth.

Rosie Flores has worked in the newspaper business for over fifteen years. She and her husband Freddy raise their children in Pecos, Texas, a small town whose atmosphere they like. She has lived all of her life in Pecos, and she writes for the *Pecos Enterprise*.

John Fooks is a staff writer for *The Texarkana Gazette*. His column is called "Days Gone By," and he writes about ordinary folks who happen to be extraordinary in special ways. His articles focus on rural and small-town life along the Texas and Arkansas border.

Since 1980, **Lora B. Garrison** has written for several Texas newspapers. She writes regularly for the *Uvalde Leader-News* with her column "Stomping Grounds." She and her husband Roger have been faithful members of the TFS since the early 1970s, and she has given many presentations over the years, in addition to serving as local arrangements coordinator for a Uvalde meeting. Her special interests are in Texas history and anthropology, and she is a public speaker in much demand on those topics.

Since 1987 **Joe Graham** has taught at Texas A&I University in Kingsville. He was born in the Big Bend and has written extensively about the folklore of that region. He is a long-time contributor to publications of the Texas Folklore Society, including editing *Hecho en Tejas: Texas-Mexican Folk Arts and Crafts*. He authored *El Rancho in South Texas: Continuity and Change from 1750* and many articles about Mexican-American folklore as found along the Mexican border.

A. C. Greene was born in 1923 in Abilene, Texas, and after service in WWII he graduated from Abilene Christian College. He served on the staff of the *Abilene Reporter-News*, ran his own bookstore and headed the journalism department at Hardin-Simmons University. He later joined the *Dallas Times-Herald*, serving as book editor and editorial page editor before being awarded a Dobie-Paisano fellowship. He currently writes a column for *The Dallas Morning News* and has written more than twenty-five books to date, including *The 50+ Best Books on Texas* and the recently released *The Santa Claus Bank Robbery*.

The publisher of *The Gilmer Mirror*, **Sarah Greene** has been a newspaper woman and journalist most of her life. She is a past president of the Texas Press Association, and she has served the Texas Folklore Society in many capacities. In recent years she has traveled throughout Texas and extensively in Europe and other parts of the world.

Born in the small community of Karnack, in Harrison County, **Haywood Hygh** studied at the University of California at Los Angeles after serving in the army. After graduate study in Berlin, he taught in high schools in California and received a master's degree from Pepperdine University. When he retired from teaching, he moved to his present home in Desoto, Texas.

Elmer Kelton, of San Angelo, Texas, is the most honored of all Western writers. Author of forty books, he is a six-time winner of the Spur Award, and has earned four Western Heritage Awards from the National Cowboy Hall of Fame. His most recent novel is *The Smiling Country*. For many years he worked as a journalist for such publications as the *San Angelo Standard-Times* and the *West Texas Livestock Weekly*.

Ernestine Sewell Linck and Charles Linck have received many awards for their books and articles. Retired professors of English from the University of Texas at Arlington and Texas A&M University at Commerce, they reside in Commerce, Texas, where they continue to write and to operate their Cow Hill Press, a small publishing company specializing in quality and rare regional works.

Stanley Marcus is Chairman Emeritus of the Neiman Marcus store. He received a B.A. degree from Harvard University and also attended Harvard Business School. A noted lecturer who publishes fine press miniature books out of The Somesuch Press, he has written *Minding the Store, Quest for the Best, His & Hers: The Fantasy World of the Neiman Marcus Catalogue*, and *The Viewpoints of Stanley Marcus*, a collection of his columns from *The Dallas Morning News*, which he has written for over a decade and continues to do so. A second collection of his columns, *Stanley Marcus from A to Z: Viewpoints Volume II* is in the offing.

Peggy McCracken has worked for twenty-eight years as a print and radio reporter and editor. She has also been managing editor for the *Pecos Enterprise*, where she is now webmaster. Her newspaper's web site won the Texas Associated Press Managing Editor's Award in its first full year on the Internet. She lives with her husband, Leon, in Pecos, Texas.

Archie P. McDonald is a professor of history at Stephen F. Austin State University and executive director of the East Texas Historical Association. He is the author or editor of approximately twenty books that deal with the history of Texas and the American Civil War and *A Cookbook: Helpful Cooking Hints for HouseHusbands of Uppity Women*. He has a heart of gold, a warped sense of humor, and a resemblance to Robert Redford.

Joyce Gibson Roach grew up in Jacksboro, Texas, attended Texas Christian University, and has been writing about Texas folklore and literature for many years. She is the author of many books, including *The Cowgirls*, and many articles. She edits anthologies, reviews books, lectures and speaks to a variety of audiences, and writes a folklore column for *The Fort Worth Star-Telegram*.

Now a professor emeritus of the Department of English, McMurry University, **Lou Rodenberger** has published essays on the experiences of her parents as rural schoolteachers between the two world wars, as well as on Texas women writers and southwestern life and literature. She is a past president of the Texas Folklore Society and West Texas Historical Association. Her most recent publication is *Texas Women Writers: A Tradition of Their Own*, co-edited with Sylvia Grider. Other works include *Her Work: Stories by Texas Women* and a critical study of West Texas writer, Jane Gilmore Rushing.

Jean Granberry Schnitz was born in Spur, Texas, and has lived in fourteen cities and towns in Texas. She graduated from Raymondville High School in 1948 and Texas A&I College in Kingsville in 1952. Married to Lew Schnitz in 1953, with three grown sons and one grandson, she now lives near Leon Springs, between Boerne and San Antonio, and is a semi-retired legal secretary. She has presented four papers to the Texas Folklore Society since 1990.

Alan Solomon has been a writer and editor for the *Houston Chronicle, Chicago Sun-Times, Philadelphia Inquirer* and the *Chicago Tribune.* A travel writer for the *Tribune* since 1994, he has received numerous awards for his journalism, including being named 1998 Lowell Thomas Travel Journalist of the Year by the Society of American Travel Writers. He lives in Chicago with his wife, freelance baseball writer Carrie Muskat.

Allan Turner, a twenty-five-year veteran in the journalistic trenches, is a lifelong student of Texas and the South. He's done stints with newspapers in Amarillo, San Antonio, and Austin and, since 1985, has been an editor and/or reporter with the *Houston Chronicle.* He is co-author, with *Chronicle* East Texas Bureau Chief Richard Stewart, of the 1998 book, *Transparent Tales: An Attic Full of Texas Ghosts.*

Jerry Turner writes regularly for the *Mexia Daily News* and *The Groesbeck Daily News.* His column is entitled "Tales of Early Texas." He received his master's degree from Abilene Christian University. He is particularly interested in the history and folklore of the Texas prison system. He teaches for Windham School District, the educational arm of TDCJ.

John O. West is the author of many books and articles, including *Mexican-American Folklore* and *José Cisneros: An Artist's Journey.* A Professor of English at the University of Texas at El Paso, he has been teaching for over fifty years and has been a member of the Texas Folklore Society since 1958. A list of his awards and honors received during his distinguished career would fill several pages.

Henry Wolff, Jr., has been a Texas journalist for most of his adult life. He has worked for the *San Angelo Standard-Times*, the *Abilene Re-*

porter-News, and *The Victoria Advocate*. In South Texas, he is a popular speaker and storyteller at history, folklore and civic gatherings. He has been with the *Advocate*, the second oldest existing newspaper in Texas, since 1963. For the last twenty years, he has been writing his column "Henry's Journal" five days a week.

Bryan Woolley is a short story writer and journalist who has published some of the best fiction and finest articles coming out of Texas in the last twenty years. His books include *The Bride Wore Crimson & Other Stories*; *Sam Bass*; and *Time and Place*. He has also published *Where Texas Meets the Sea: A Coastal Portrait*. He writes for *The Dallas Morning News*.

Index

A

adobe, source, 120
adobe houses, 118–122
adobe mud, 121–122
ague, 44
Aguilar, Federico, Jr., 34
Akins, Corbett, 75–77, 78–79
Albuquerque Journal, The, 13, 212
Alexander, Alger "Texas," 134
Allison, Clay, 22, 154
Allred, James V., 185
Alpine, 70, 213
Alpine Avalanche, The, 9
Amarillo, 184
armadillo, 93–95; eating, 94; racing, 94; reproduction of, 95
Andy's Diner (Fredericksburg), 208, 209
Armendariz, Luis, 122

B

Bandera (TX), 206
Bean, Judge Roy, 28–29
bestiaries, 115
Biffle, Kent, 6
Boatwright, Mody, 80
Bohanan, Walter. *See* Girvin Social Club
Bouquet of Biscuits, A, 220–221
braggart, 139–140
Brewer, J. Mason, 3, 168–171; firsts of, 169; publications of, 170
Broken Spoke Cafe (Austin), 6, 207, 208

Brooks, Edna, 27
Butterfield Overland Mail, 197

C

Caprock Sun (Lubbock), 11
Campion, William, 34
Castle Gap, 195–205; massacre at, 197–198
catarrh, 44
Catholic Cross Cache, 203–204
chicken-fried steak, 206–212; recipe, 209–210, 211–212
Clarendon News, The, 186
Cleburne, 181
Cleo, 164–166
Columbus, Christopher, 89–92
Commerce Journal, The, 43, 171
country-fried steak, 207. *See also* chicken-fried steak
cow chip tea recipe, 145–146
Crabb, Brett, 183
Craig, Hiram G., 106–107, 109
Crane, 195
Crazy Women in the Rafters, 214
cross-cut saw, 38
Crum, Jay, 55
curandero. See folk healers

D

Daily Sentinel, The, 87, 89, 92
Dallas, Stella, 52
Dallas Morning News, The, 29, 74, 79, 107, 110, 112, 114, 117

Dallas Times Herald, The, 15, 141, 177

"The Day Before Christmas" (poem), 187–188

Dearen, Patrick, 18, 20, 220–221

Degh, Linda, 5

Dobie, J. Frank, 157, 169, 197

Dorsey, Tommy, 128

down beat magazine, 128

E

Eagle-News, 180, 183

East Texas State University, 168

Eats, a Folk History of Texas Foods, 6, 207

Ellwood, Brooks, 106

erysipelas, 44

Estes, Billy Sol, 156

evil eye, 161–163

F

family stories, 80

Ferguson, Miriam "Ma," 56

Ferro, Dickie Dell, 28

Fifth Ward (Houston), 133

folk beliefs, 158–163; defined, 158

folk healers, 142–148, 159

folk medicines, 45–46; 142–152, 160–163

folk poet, 15

folk poetry, 14–15; defined, 15

folk religion, 159

folklore, defined, 3, 5; reported in newspapers, 5

Folklore and the Mass Media, 5

"Formula for Success" (poem), 193–194

Fort Davis, Texas, 7

Fort Leaton, 119, 122–123

Fort Leaton State Historical Park, 122

Fort Worth Star-Telegram, 36, 46, 50, 54, 84, 162

Fourth Ward (Houston), 131

Frazer, Bud, 154

G

"Garage Sales" (poem), 190–191

Garner, John Nance, 203

Gary High School, 75, 77–78

Giddings, 106–107

Gilmer, 96–101

Gilmer Mirror, The, 101

Girvin Social Club, The, 26–27

Goodnight, Charles, 17–18

Goodnight-Loving Trail, 20, 197

Goodrich, Lloyd, 24–26

"Granny" and her peas, 66–69

Green, Ray, 34

greenhorn. *See* newcomer

Grey, Zane, 17

Guzman, Isaac, 13

H

Hadacol, 143

Hill Country Cupboard (Johnson City), 208

Hobbs News-Sun, 1

Hopkins, Samuel "Lightnin,'" 126, 132–133

Hornung Hatchery calendar, 61–62

horse apples, 42, 43

Horsehead Crossing, 20, 21, 195, 196

Houston Chronicle, 123, 136

Houston Jazz Appreciation Society, 128

Houston Press, 106–107

"How to Write a Poem" (poem), 192–193

Howard, Pauline, 181–182

humor and frontier life, 137–141

I

I'll Gather My Geese, 73

J

Jasper, Pat, 120, 121
Jeff Davis County Mountain Dispatch, 7,8
Jefferson Street (Dallas), 12
Jones, Buddy, 102–105
Jones, Elgin "Punk,"18
Jones, "Little Hat," 129
Jones, Lorenzo, 52
Jones, Skeet, 22

K

Karnack (TX), 146–150
Kelton, Elmer, 9, 23, 214, 218
King, Lincoln, 78
Kingsville-Bishop Record News, 194
Kirtley, Bacil F., 33–34
Ku Klux Klan, 56

L

La Llorona, 30–36; and European origin, 34; other versions of story, 31; and water, 33
Leaton, Benjamin. *See* Fort Leaton
Leita, Raymond, 59
Linck, Ernestine Sewell, 6, 207
Lipscomb, Mance, 126
Livingston, Skinny, 60
Loblolly magazine (Gary High School), 75, 77–78
Lomax, John A., 137; and Alan, 136
Lonesome Dove, 20
Longley, Bill, 106–112; execution, 107, 109–110; faked letters from, 111; grave, 106; last words, 109
Longley, Campbell, 110–112
Looney, Morgan H., 96–101
Looney School, 96–101

Lopp, William A., 45, 49
Lost Maples Cafe (Utopia), 208
Loving County, 24–26
Lubbock Avalanche-Journal, The, 10–11
Lubbock County Independent, 11
Lucille, TX, 81
Lupercalia, as source of Valentine's Day, 88
Lynch, Mrs. Don, 63

M

mal de ojo, 161–163; treatment, 161–162
Marathon, 71
Marks, Crystal, 9
Marshall News Messenger, 152
Maximilian's treasure, 198–202
"Maybe Next Year" (poem), 188
McClellan, Bill, 107, 109
McCormick, Mack, 124–136
McKinney Courier-Gazette, 57
McMurtry, Larry, 20
Meinzer, Wyman, 10–11
Mentone, 24
Mexia Daily News, 95
Midland Reporter-Telegram, The, 205
Miller, Jim, 154
Miriam, 57
Monument (NM), 4
moon, and planting, 66
Moore, Rance, 166
Mountain Dispatch. See Jeff Davis County Mountain Dispatch

N

National Cowboy Symposium, The, 11
newcomer as subject of jokes, 138–139

Newland, Cliff, 203–205

newspapers, large circulation, 12–13; small-town, 7; travel sections, 12–13

O

Orozco, Carmen, 118–123

O.S.T. Cafe (Bandera), 208

P

Patterson, Frank and N.Q., 166–167

Patterson, Paul, 9, 21, 22–24, 196, 204; biography, 216–221; honored by peers, 213–215; publications of, 214

Pearce, T.M., 14–15

Pecos, 153–154, 213, 216; origin of name, 23–24

Pecos Bill, 21

Pecos Enterprise, 215, 221

Pecos River, 17–24, 28

Pecos River shelter paintings, 29

poetry, folk. *See* folk poetry

Potter, Dadie, 70

Presidio (TX), 119, 122

Pringle, Burl and Frankie, 27

prison work songs, 134–136

R

Ramsey, Buck, 213

Randel, Jo Stewart, 184–186

Rankin, Billy, 196–200, 205

rattlesnakes, 181–183; eating, 182; handlers, 182–183

rayon, 185–186

Red Bluff, 25

Redford, 118–119

Redding, Gid, 22–23, 219–220

Reeves, Lois, 60

Riggs, Barney, 154

Rippamonti, Vincent, Jr., 58–59

Roach, Joyce, 6, 207

Roach, Nessye Mae, 8

Roberts, Oran M., 96, 98

Roosevelt, Franklin Delano, 184–186

roosters, 59–65, 68

root doctors, 142–148

rural schools, 80

S

St. John, Bob, 12

salt cedar, 25

San Angelo Daily Standard, 204

San Angelo Standard-Times, 164

"Santa Fe" pianists, 131

scarlet fever, cure for, 101

Schnitz, Jean Granberry, 16

Sears and Roebuck Catalogue, 46

Shafter, Colonel William, 4, 7

Shaw, Robert, 126, 131

Six Myths of Our Time, 14

smallpox, cure for, 101

Smiling Country, The, 9

Solomon, Alan, 6

Stamps Quartet, 51

Stevenson, Coke, 164

Stillwell, Hallie, 70–74

stomach disorders, 44–45

"Such Weather!" (poem), 189–190

Sul Ross College, 216

superstition, 158

Swift, Smokey, 195, 200, 203

T

Talbot family, 172–176

Terlingua chili wars, 73

Texarkana Gazette, The, 105

Texas Cowboy Poetry Gathering, 213–215

Texas Folklife Resources, 120

"Texian Boys" (song), 140–141

Thomas, Henry, 125, 130–131

Thompson, Thomas Jefferson, 45–46
Tournament of Roses, 86
Threadgill's (Austin), 209
Tubb, Ernest, 51
"The TV Tube Syndrome" (poem),
    189

U
urban legend, 4, 12
Uvalde Leader-News, 69

V
Valadez, Alfonso, 178–180
versos, 15
Victoria Advocate, The, 59, 61, 63,
    65

W
Warner, Marina, 14
weather signs, 113–114
Weeping Woman. *See* La Llorona

West, John O., 158
West of the Pecos, 17
West Texas Livestock Weekly, 157
White, Annetta, 207, 209–210
White, James M., 6, 210
Whitehead, Dr., 143–144
Wight, Mary Lee, 35
Williams, Dr. F.E., 147–148
Williams, R.G., 135
Wills, Bob, 6, 210
Wise, Don, 209
women and Western life, 8
Woolley, Bryan, 6

Y
Yates Oil Field, 27–28
"Yesterday, Today, and Tomorrow"
    (poem), 191–192

Z
Zozobra (Old Man Gloom), 10